THE FREEDOM MASTER PLAN

Put Your Mission, Movement
and Message on the Map

For Vegan and Ethical Experts,
Influencers and Entrepreneurs

Mitali Deypurkaystha
www.thefreedommasterplan.com

COPYRIGHT

To Isha and Kali, you had no idea how your presence would change the course of my life - you transformed me

CONTENTS

TABLE OF FIGURES

THANK YOU FOR READING
THE FREEDOM MASTER PLAN

This book is an actionable and practical guide showing you how to achieve freedom from:

- selling and sales anxiety
- lead generation burnout
- frustrating clients
- working long hours to hit revenue and impact goals

You can do this by leveraging an authority-building business book.

If you don't have a business book yet, this book's digital companion is an excellent place to start, where you can get two free gifts designed to get your book to market as fast and professionally as possible:

- 5 Steps to Writing and Publishing Your Business Book
- 21 Questions You Must Ask a Nonfiction Business Book Publisher Before You Sign a Contract

Go to:

- www.thefreedommasterplan.com

I'm also including a bunch of free resources at the companion site, plus work-sheets and exercises mentioned in this book. Those are all available from one handy link, as my thanks to you:

- www.thefreedommasterplan.com/free-resources

REVIEWS

I read The Freedom Master Plan from cover to cover, and Mitali gave me some diamond advice. I've seen the ideas in her book being lived out in reality, and I imitated her and became an international bestselling author myself.

It's not one of those business books where you're left missing the how. She gives it all away. The Freedom Master Plan is an easy read, logical and very doable advice. I did it, and I've experienced 1000X ROI.

Heather Landex - Vegan Entrepreneur in Food Service,
Inclusive Food Service Ltd

The Freedom Master Plan is the ultimate guide for coaches, consultants and other professionals who want to share their expertise through writing a deeply impactful book. Written with clear and engaging examples and case studies, The Freedom Master Plan demonstrates actionable tips for how your book can create a greater impact for your business, magnetize your ideal clients, eliminate sales anxiety and empower you to become an authority in your field.

As a new author, I have found Mitali's wisdom and expertise to be an invaluable guide on my path.

Angela Crawford, Ph.D. – Psychologist,
Vegan Lifestyle Educator and Author

It is one thing to write a business book. It's another thing to write a successful business book that drives your business forward, opening up new connections, possibilities and revenue streams. The Freedom Master Plan is full of valuable insights drawn from the author's personal experiences in the writing and publishing industries, pointing out what not to do as well as how to get the best results. She provides easily actionable information and explains exactly why each of her pointers make good commercial sense.

If you understand the value of becoming a business author and thought-leader, this book is a must-read to get you going on the right track. Don't waste your valuable time – read and study The Freedom Master Plan to maximize your chances of success.

Amanda Redman, MA - Chartered Financial Planner (vegan-owned business)

The Freedom Master Plan really inspired me. Mitali knows her stuff, and I recommend any (vegan, plant-based, eco, ethical, etc.) business founder who wants to make a difference read this book!

Will Saunders - Founder and Creative Director, Good Will Studios

Mitali is an incredible author coach. So it should be no surprise that her book, The Freedom Master Plan, shows that she practices what she preaches! Her book is inspiring and full of valuable information for those with an inkling that writing a book will help them boost their career, whatever it may be.

I loved working with her, I thoroughly enjoyed reading her book, and I'm excited that we share a passion and commitment to a vegan lifestyle.

Bobbi Giudicelli - CEO/Co-founder of Read The Ingredients (whole-food plant-based breakfasts)

Mitali Deypurkaystha's brilliant, easy-to-read book, The Freedom Master Plan, will help you multiply sales so that they soar, thereby freeing yourself and freeing many animals.

Marvin Ginsberg - Vegan Life Coach

The Freedom Master Plan is hugely inspiring to read. Before reading it, I didn't know how to start my author's journey. But after finishing it, I was left feeling as though I had both the focus and drive to write a book. You can tell she's done her time in the book industry and has a huge amount to give in terms of guidance and insight.

Chris Bryant - Chris Bryant Creative Design
(vegan-owned business)

At last! A book that's easy to read and makes so much sense you feel moved to take action. The Freedom Master Plan is the ultimate guide for vegan professionals who want to share their expertise through writing an impactful book.

I'm at the very early stages of my journey as an author, but this book has inspired me to keep going, and I know I will be a published author with my fellow vegan Mitali's help in the not too distant future!

Jill Bennett - Plant-Based Health Advocate
for Living Beautifully with Jill Bennett,
Radio Presenter, Podcast Host

Mitali's writing style is down to earth and to the point, just what you want as a busy consultant. There's no messing about. You'll be sold by the time you've reached the end of chapter one. Each page is gold. Even if you've heard some of this stuff before, you've not heard it from Mitali. She is one person you want to have on your side.

Coral McCloud – Branding and Design Consultant,
Rebel Mumma (vegan-owned business)

This fabulous book offers powerful insights into how to become an authority in your field. Every paragraph is clearly written and contains profound nuggets of wisdom. Start reading The Freedom Master Plan, and you'll find yourself looking for free time to read more.

Mitali couldn't have made the path to business success more understandable. If you're ready to commit to making something great happen in your life, Mitali's book, The Freedom Master Plan, is a fantastic place to start.

Sam Roblett - CEO of Zebra Admin,
Online Business Support for Vegan, Plant-Based and Ethical Businesses

As a vegan business owner with a unique story to tell, I've wanted to write a book for years. My story ties in with my reason for making the connection to veganism. Who better to learn from than Mitali? I decided to read The Freedom Master Plan. I found the book to be informative and inspiring. It was easy to navigate and has made me confident that I will be a published author one day.

Hayley Cooper - Founder of Wild Dreams Hospitality,
Consulting and Recruitment (vegan-owned business)

In a world where being an expert just doesn't cut it, writing your own book truly helps vegan entrepreneurs become 'thought leaders' in their niche. And there is no one who is more adept and qualified at helping you take this journey than Mitali. And the proof is in this book!

It is simple, concise and packed with content that will give you value right away! Read this book and connect with Mitali right away. It will be your best investment ever.

Trevor Banerjee - Vegan Business Mentor,
The Freedom Switch

Wow! If you want to know how to make your book work hard for you, I highly recommend reading The Freedom Master Plan. This book gave me so much insight into how to utilize a book as a marketing tool, as well as countless marketing tips. If you're ready to commit to making something great happen in your life, Mitali's book is a great place to start. Enjoy reading!

**Sanita Kaur - Business Development Manager
and author of Healthy Hacks Healthy Habits Blog**

It is a pleasure recommending Mitali's book, and I do so wholeheartedly. As a self-published author of ethical fiction books, The Freedom Master Plan provides me with all the right tips and tools for igniting inner motivation and outreaching into the challenging publishing market, reaching further readers, spreading the message, and inviting valuable success.

**M.C Ronen - Author of ethical suspense books,
The Liberation Trilogy**

The Freedom Master Plan is pure wisdom straight from the mouth of someone who has reached the goals you're working so hard to achieve. While other books have insights, this book gives you the straight-up truth from those who have actually done it. Stop looking for better information—you'll find it right here! I have enjoyed reading every bit of this book.

**Lina Kochanske - Holistic Wellness Coaching at A-Zen Wellness Ltd
(vegan-owned business)**

During the long lockdowns, The Freedom Master Plan became a roadmap that gave me the confidence and tools to reinvent myself and become a best-selling author and speaker. Mitali Deypurkaystha couldn't have made the pathways to success in publishing more straightforward. I especially liked how she provided several strategies so you could find the best approach for your personality and set your own goals. This book motivated me, built my confidence and focused me on success. It's the only book you need to transform your life.

Todd Sinclair - public speaker, travel specialist, podcaster, and author of the Rebel Vegan trilogy

Every life is an adventure unfolding, a book in the making, one with love, joys, hurt, sorrows, compassion, resilience, heartbreak, healing and, most of all, learning. If you're ready to make a commitment to make something great happen, if you're ready to share the message of what you stand for, and how you're navigating your life and your mission, Mitali's book, The Freedom Master Plan, is a great place to start.

I've never read a book that's as packed with hands-on, step-by-step information while showing you how to showcase your writing, expression, creativity and freedom and more like this one. This book should be required reading for anyone in business.

Nivi Jaswal, MBA, NBC-HWC, Founder - The Virsa Foundation, Ethical Investor and Vegan Activist

FOREWORD

In 2014 I was ready to reinvent myself. After 17 years as a journalist in an ever-changing media landscape, I was trying to find a new purpose and direction.

I was curious about entrepreneurship and started networking with business owners. I enjoyed learning about their challenges and sharing my insights into getting featured in the media. But something was missing.

I wasn't feeling passionate about helping just any random business owner. My good friend, Melissa, asked me who I truly wanted to serve. I immediately replied, "Vegan entrepreneurs."

Vegan since 1997, I'm committed to doing my part to create a world where animals are no longer commodified, harmed or killed for human consumption. A world in which humans are not exploited. A world in which we care for the planet instead of destroying it.

At the time, I was known in the vegan and animal rights community as a journalist who wrote about social justice issues, including animal advocacy.

How could I now position myself as an authority in the vegan ethical business space and carve out a new career?

At 3 AM one morning, I sat bolt upright in bed, exhilarated. I'd suddenly had the idea to write a book on how to start and grow a vegan business.

A year later, Vegan Ventures: Start and Grow an Ethical Business was out in the world, the first-ever book of its kind. Since then, I've spoken at events across the globe, moderated panels and been featured in a variety of media (including a regular column for Forbes for an entire year). I've created a PR consultancy, an online course and a copywriting business to help vegan entrepreneurs, coaches, consultants and creatives raise their profiles.

Writing and publishing a book made all this possible. It made me one of the key 'go-to' people in the vegan and ethical sector. It gave me authority and credibility. Invitations continue to come my way to participate in relevant summits, panels, events and other collaborations, all of which generate leads and sales for my business.

This is why Mitali Deypurkaystha's book, The Freedom Master Plan: Put Your Mission, Movement and Message on the Map, is a no-brainer for any vegan or ethical professional who wants to become the authority in their field. Mitali not only sets out all the reasons and benefits of being a published author, but she also shows you how to reap these benefits by correctly leveraging your book.

You may think that all you need to do is focus on social media, paid ads, SEO or PR to grow your business. These are all important. But guess what? Being a published author helps you with all these. For example, you can repurpose most of your book into social media and blog content.

And you become much more interesting to journalists when you're an author. When the media are looking for experts to comment or feature, there's unlikely to be a shortage of professionals in your field. As an author, you have far more credibility and are more likely to be trusted by journalists.

If you're reading this, you likely have an inkling that you have a book 'inside you.' Or you know you want to be a published author but are unsure how it will help you grow your business.

You're in the right place. Mitali is an award-winning ghostwriter and copywriter who's helped her clients earn millions of dollars by leveraging their books.

Becoming an author alone won't necessarily improve your bottom line. You need to know how to make your book work for you. In The Freedom Master Plan, she shares exactly how her big-name clients used their books as a marketing tool.

Mitali shows you how to do just that so that 'selling' becomes effortless. You'll learn how being a published author helps you easily attract your ideal clients, referrals and collaborative partners.

As stated in Vegan Ventures, my mission is 'vegan world domination, one business at a time.' More vegan entrepreneurs writing smart, strategic books is a powerful way to make this happen. You couldn't be in better hands than Mitali's to start your author journey.

Katrina Fox - Media/PR Consultant, Speaker
Author of Vegan Ventures: Start and Grow an Ethical Business

INTRODUCTION

About Me

Hi, I'm Mitali. To date, I've ghostwritten seven authority-building books that earned over $6.5 million for my clients in additional business revenue. I'm also responsible for generating over $2 million through sales pages, adverts and e-mail marketing as a copywriter.

After working with 20+ marketers, entrepreneurs, experts and influencers across different specialties in the last ten years, I've discovered that the piece of content that makes the biggest difference and turns you into a magnet for success is a professionally written and published book.

I'm the owner of The Vegan Publisher, a 100% vegan-owned and operated book consulting company, and the Let's Tell Your Story publishing imprint, both dedicated to transforming vegan, plant-based, ethical, sustainable, B Corp, cruelty-free, eco-conscious and social experts, influencers and entrepreneurs into bestselling authors.

I'm known as 'The Authority Creator', enabling these inspiring people to effortlessly amplify their visibility and profits, attract ideal clients, investors, donors, speaking opportunities and even national and international press. All while changing the world, one book at a time.

I show them how to write a business book that is designed to help them gain freedom from:

- selling and sales anxiety
- lead generation burnout
- frustrating clients
- working long hours to hit revenue and impact goals

At the same time, they're building their authority, gaining expert status in their field, becoming a respected thought leader, and putting their mission, movement and message on the map. If this is also your goal, you're in the right place.

Why I Wrote This Book

In 2009, I adopted a rescue cat who dramatically changed my life. For the first time, I witnessed intelligence and sentience beyond what I was led to believe animals were capable of showing.

I realized I was duped into believing animals are dumb as this suits certain industries. I became vegan in 2012.

In early 2021, it dawned on me that I was almost halfway through my life. And my dream of a vegan-normal world will not be realized unless the voices of vegan and ethical business owners became louder.

Over the last ten years, I've been lucky enough to meet some incredible vegan and ethical experts and entrepreneurs who have furthered my understanding of the necessity of plant-based living. I've witnessed three distinct routes someone may take where their consciousness is raised to the point that becoming plant-based or vegan becomes inevitable. One route is the realization that animals are far more sentient than we thought (my personal route).

Other people come into the vegan and ethical space after realizing that it's the best solution for the planet. Over the last few years, I've met respected academics who explained that animal-based food production causes great damage to the environment, such as water shortages and deforestation from farming, greenhouse gases from livestock, and dead parts of oceans from agricultural pollution.

Others still become aware of the health implications of animal product consumption. I've always questioned the consumption of dairy. Since the 60s and 70s, "breast is best" has been something many people in the West heard while growing up. If breast milk is so perfectly designed for an infant that even the mightiest of food companies can't fully replicate in their formula milk, what is cow's milk perfectly designed for? Not us!

I've been lucky enough to meet some incredible plant-based nutritionists. They've explained to me that in the next few decades, the scandal that will arise from the misinformation spewed out by the dairy industry will dwarf the Big Tobacco lawsuit in the early noughties.

Furthering my understanding of the different routes into veganism, I've met some fascinating people who've explained the links between animal rights and feminism, veganism and the LGTBQIA+ community, and Big Food and Big Pharma. Only very recently did I learn of the harrowing links between African Americans and fast food companies, prisons and slaughterhouses.

It doesn't matter which route you took. You could be a vegan health coach whose mission is to stop people from developing diabetes, heart disease and other illnesses wrongly labeled as the inevitable effects of aging. You could be an ethical financial advisor whose goal is to redirect funds currently going to companies that promote activities that lead to deforestation.

Activism through business is the key to 'veganizing' the world. When people are given viable alternatives to products created through exploitation (of animals, the environment or humans), most make the ethical choice.

However, according to the US Bureau of Labor, 20% of small businesses fail in the first year and 50% by five years. These statistics are replicated in nearly all Western countries.

The reasons given for these failure rates are:

1. little or no selling skills
2. little or no lead generation or marketing skills

I found that most vegan and ethical entrepreneurs start a business because they're passionate about making a difference in the world. So they strike out on their own and build a business around their skills. What they don't expect is the need to learn a whole other skill set; sales, marketing and lead generation.

In addition, vegan and ethical businesses have the extra strain of making ethical choices that are unfairly more expensive, adding further pressure.

I resolved to use my skills and expertise to help as many vegan and ethical business owners, experts, influencers and entrepreneurs as possible boost their visibility, authority, sales and profits by becoming published authors.

Additionally, I have an affinity with coaches, consultants, mentors and therapists. I needed a lot of help for various issues since the age of 19, such as weight, addiction, mental health, business and career.

- I went from a UK size 20 (US 16) to a UK size 10 (US 6) because of a nutrition consultant and fitness coach.
- I went from hopelessly addicted to amphetamines to completely clean for 20 years because of an addiction counselor and life coach.
- I went from a soul-destroying call center job to running my own copywriting and ghostwriting business because of a business coach.

Even now, I have a consultant, a coach and a therapist to help me navigate this strange thing called life. I could not have achieved any of this without these amazing people throughout the years.

They kept me focused, kept me accountable, and in one case, kept me alive.

It's why I love working with coaches and consultants and why you'll notice that a lot of the strategies in the book are skewed toward service-based business owners.

However, don't worry if you're a product-based entrepreneur or run an organization, such as a charity, nonprofit, etc. Throughout this book, there are numerous strategies that can easily be adapted to suit your particular needs. After all, which business or organization doesn't need more eyeballs on them?

Who This Book is For

This book is designed for vegan and ethical leaders, entrepreneurs, experts and influencers who have either written a business book, or would like to write one, but they're unsure how it can help their business or organization.

You're living your dream of running a business, but are you doing (and not enjoying) sales calls or lead generation? Perhaps you have a few nightmare clients. Maybe you're working too long to hit your revenue goals.

I will guide you through exactly how you can leverage a book to gain freedom from these problems.

Leverage is:

- the reason a coach with two years' experience can earn higher fees than coaches with ten or more years' experience
- how experts, influencers and entrepreneurs can build a passive income
- why speakers can secure more well-paid speaking gigs
- the reason why a rookie coach is able to set up his entire social media lead generation on autopilot and he never has to write a single piece of content again
- how anyone can position themselves as a thought leader in their industry

And now you're about to discover how you can leverage a business book too.

Who This Book is Not For

This book is not for you if you want to make a living from book sales. I want to state emphatically that selling your book is absolutely the worst way to make money. If there is just one thing you take away from this book then let it be this: the book is *not* the business!

Let me break it down for you. The average business book sells around 3,000 copies. Not per week or per month or per year. That's total. 3,000 copies, total.

The average royalty rate is about 8% for paperback books. If you sold your book at a reasonable $14.99, you earn approximately $1.60 per book. For 3,000 books, you earn a little under $4,800.

The book is not the business!

Total. $4,800 *total* earnings. If you think that's a good return on your time and effort, you need to raise your ambitions.

If you go down the self-publishing route, you'll make more money per book as a publishing company will not eat most of your profits. However, self-publishing means a lot of upfront costs for editors, designers, etc. This is without any guarantees your book will sell well.

If you want to be the next J.K. Rowling and make a fortune with a book, then The Freedom Master Plan is not for you.

I have no experience of the traditional book business. I have no idea how those books are profitable all on their own. However, I do know how to make books profitable.

You have to think of your book as the key to the treasure and not the treasure itself. Your future clients, strategic partners, investors, affiliates, etc., are behind closed doors. Not only that, they're behind doors that they barricaded.

We're bombarded with marketing messages. Anywhere between 4,000 and 10,000 times per day, according to Forbes estimates. Is it any wonder you mass-delete e-mails and your brain learns to ignore ads? Anything to rid of the clutter.

Nearly all business owners face this problem when trying to get their message out there. But a seismic shift happens when you have a book.

Suddenly, you're not just a salesperson selling your products or services. You're an expert author. You're not sending out marketing messages that are to be tuned out and ignored. Your messages are now words of sage advice.

Your prospect is no longer doing you a favor by granting you their precious time. You're doing them a favor. You're now a trusted advisor. Nothing opens doors for you the way a book does.

Not only that, your book is a marketing tool that outlasts all other forms of marketing. TV or radio adverts are gone in 30 seconds. E-mails are deleted after a glance, if they are lucky enough to be opened in the first place.

Newspapers? There's a phrase in the UK. "Today's news is tomorrow's chip paper," proving the transitory status of newspapers. (For US readers, here in the UK we call French fries chips. Traditionally they were bagged up and served in sheets of yesterday's newspaper).

But we collect books.

We create bookshelves and cases to display them in. We build libraries to house them in to be shared with our community. What other written medium do you know where any of this happens so readily?

My expertise comes from working closely with marketers, entrepreneurs, experts and influencers. It comes from writing lots of different kinds of sales copy for them over five years. And I discovered that the sales copy with the biggest impact on sales, is a book.

Not just any kind of book. A book that is specifically written to build their authority and designed to be given away instead of being sold. Don't worry though. I don't advocate giving your book to anyone and everyone.

Inside The Freedom Master Plan, you'll discover tried and tested strategies my clients use to leverage their books by first determining who their target audience is. This negates the cost of them giving their book away for free. When they do give their book away, the chances of a great return on investment are high.

Other strategies involve selling your book at a low price to cover your costs. For example, if you're featured by a local newspaper, you can encourage interested readers to reach out by directing them to your website for a copy of your book at a discount.

Here, with a local paper, the readership could be diverse. By selling your book at-cost, you mitigate any money wasted on people who will never be a good fit.

As mentioned earlier, I've written seven business books that are responsible for over $6.5 million in additional business revenue to-date for my clients. And yet, I doubt any of them made more than a few thousand dollars from selling their books.

Instead, they used their books to grow their business. To increase the influence they have on their target market. To increase fees without complaints. To create secondary and even tertiary income streams. And to become seen as a force to be reckoned with, reaching thought leadership status.

Is this what you want for yourself? If so, stick around.

What This Book Covers

Over the next five chapters, I'm going to cover what you need to focus on in order to leverage a business book to gain freedom from the common problems most business owners face, and become an authority in your field.

Leverage Your Book to Get Dream Clients

Many entrepreneurs start their business because they want the freedom to choose who they work with, and yet they end up attracting frustrating, nightmarish clients.

I'll get to the heart of why this happens, how you can use your book to turn away those people while attracting dream clients, and generate a steady flow of dream clients to your business. You can even download my Dream Client Worksheet to pinpoint your perfect clients.

Leverage Your Book to Increase Your Profits

All service-based business owners would love to increase their fees, but they fear losing clients. Not only that, they're dependent on selling knowledge by the hour. That means taking time out of their business is tricky because as soon as they stop working, they stop earning.

I show you how to leverage a book to increase your fees without losing clients, even gaining clients. You will also discover how to build passive income streams (along with a handy mind map) so that your income does not completely dry up when you stop working.

Leverage Your Book to Remove Sales Anxiety

Selling is scary! Just the thought of trying to convince someone to see the value in what you offer is frightening. Most of us hate being pushy and we hate rejection.

I teach you how to use your book to sell for you, enabling your prospects to see the value in what you do without feeling pushy, eliminating all sales anxiety and fear of rejection.

Leverage Your Book to Generate Qualified Leads

Keeping a pipeline of prospects warm and progressing is a difficult process, which means many entrepreneurs bounce from feast to famine continually in their business.

I share how you can use a business book to generate constant streams of warm leads to you both online and offline, encourage other people to generate leads for you, and gain freedom from the feast and famine cycle for good.

Summary: Leverage Your Book for Thought Leadership

Thought leadership is not just a buzzword. When someone is a thought leader, everything in their business, from lead generation and sales to attracting dream clients, investors, the media, etc., becomes so much easier.

I will give you the easiest way to become a sought-after, respected thought leader and authority, along with my foolproof Authority Catalyst Speech Template that will enable you to give powerful speeches, even if you've never given one before.

Bonus Chapter: How to Write an Authority-Building Book

Although this book is about how to leverage a business book, I know there will be many people who are not authors already and are inspired to write their first book after reading The Freedom Master Plan. I share the basic steps of planning and writing a business book that can give you freedom from selling, generate leads for you and position you as an authority and future thought leader. I'll also walk you through the editing, publishing and promotional steps of your book journey.

How to Use This Book

Please read the chapters in order.

You may want to go straight to a particular chapter because you feel one of the problems is the most pressing in your business. Don't do this.

You'll progress faster if you read the chapters in order as each one builds on the previous.

I recommend getting your favorite notepad handy before the next chapter. Books, like all other content, can only help you if you take action. Creating a handy list of strategies you want to use will motivate you to take action.

I provide tools and resources throughout the book, such as workbooks, templates and mind maps. Make sure you use them as these are designed to make it easier for you to implement the strategies. To save you going through the book to find each resource, I created a useful, at-a-glance Resources page at the back of the book.

At the end of each chapter, you will find a multiple choice quiz (answers at the end of the book). Make sure you do these tests as it will allow you to determine how much information you retained.

Remember, reading this book won't give you the results you want. You need to take action, and you can only take action if you retain the information.

Furthermore, I'm keen to help you as much as possible.

I'm living my life's mission as 'The Authority Creator' for vegan and ethical experts, influencers, and entrepreneurs, helping them dramatically increase their visibility, authority and profits by becoming published authors.

I invite you to join my mission to create an army of conscious, ethical thought leaders through publishing, so our screams to end the exploitation of animals, humans, and the environment will become too loud to be ignored.

To that end, please do contact me if you want to work with me. My contact details are at the end of the book.

Let's Go!

It's time for you to finally attract the leads, clients, investors, media attention, etc., you always wanted. Get the recognition and earnings you deserve, and experience the freedom you desire in your business.

(Please note: I mention several of my former clients in this book. As their ghostwriter, I legally cannot name them due to the standard non-disclosure agreements. Pseudonyms are used to protect their identity.)

CHAPTER 1

LEVERAGE YOUR BOOK
TO GET DREAM CLIENTS

Many service-based entrepreneurs start their businesses to experience the freedom of choosing the best clients. Instead, many end up struggling with lazy, unmotivated and frustrating clients.

Perhaps they're fearful of rejecting a paying client because they need the money? Maybe they feel it's their responsibility to transform their clients, *no matter what*. After all, that's what they're paid to do, right?

Wrong. They can only show their clients the road. The choice to walk down it is up to each client.

There's an old saying, "God helps those who help themselves." Nobody can be helped if they're not willing to help themselves.

You need clients who resonate with why you do what you do. They also need to have a clear understanding of why they're unsatisfied, what transformations they want, and how you can help them.

Otherwise, you're sucked into trying to change people who *think* they want to change, but are not prepared to actually change.

In this chapter:

- you'll discover how to use your business book to attract your dream clients
- you'll learn how your book can encourage these dream clients to refer you to other potential dream clients

- you'll find out how your book can help dissuade potential clients who are a bad fit, getting rid of them before they have the chance to exasperate you
- and you'll get my Dream Client Worksheet to help you discover who is your dream client

Get ready to experience the freedom of working with people who are a joy to help.

How Do I Attract Dream Clients?

A wise mentor told me that there are only two types of problems in the world: information problems and motivation problems.

An example of an information problem would be vacationing in a foreign country. You don't realize that everyone drives on the other side of the road. You step out onto a road and a car almost runs you over.

There are only two types of problems in the world: information problems and motivation problems.

You now have the information you need to look the opposite way while in this foreign country. The problem was an information problem. Once you had the right information, the problem was solved.

Motivation problems, on the other hand, are never solved by providing information. Take, for example, a smoker. Lecturing them on how they are damaging their lungs and putting themselves at risk of cancer rarely makes them stop.

They know the risks. Supplying them with more information has little effect on them. Instead, you're probably creating problems in the relationship. They have a motivation problem. Until they find a motivating reason to quit, they will carry on smoking.

The difficulty arises when your potential clients fall somewhere between the two types of problems. In most cases, they need the correct information, but they also need motivation.

This is why fitness coaches exist, for example. Most people know they need to exercise to lose weight. Yes, they may need some information on the correct way to do specific exercises. But what they really want is someone to hold them accountable.

People hire fitness coaches because they're motivated to lose weight and get fit. They want someone who will keep them from slacking off.

In the same way, your dream clients are those who have a certain level of motivation to make changes in their life, business or whatever field you work in. They need guidance, the right information, accountability and a touch of inspiration to tip the balance.

Are Your Clients Coachable?

Have you ever gone through the torture of running a survey to screen potential clients? Good news. Your book offers a very natural way to screen for dream clients, and you never need to touch a spreadsheet.

When someone decides they want to learn something or need a solution for a problem, they have many choices. They can Google. They can post on Facebook. They can go to an online forum. Or a myriad of other online places.

There's nothing wrong with any of this, but here's the stark truth: literally anyone can set up a website or blog and start giving advice without any fact-checking. Anyone can reply with their opinion on Facebook, regardless of any qualifications.

What are the chances of real expertise?

Now let's compare that to someone who goes to Amazon and invests in a book. Or they get in their car and drive to their nearest bookstore for information that solves their problem. How is this person different from the previous person?

- They're discerning and want their information from credible sources.
- They have respect for authority and qualifications.
- They're willing to invest time, money and effort for the right guidance.
- They take their time making decisions instead of being impulsive.
- They're motivated as they're willing to put in the effort to find solutions.

Read the above list again. Does this book reader also sound like a dream client? Because they are! People who demonstrate the above qualities are always the perfect clients.

Whenever I meet happy, fulfilled coaches, consultants and other service-based business owners, they have clients who are book buyers and readers. This is no coincidence.

Also, depending on the type of service you offer, you may need a client to digest a lot of material. A book reader proves that they're able and willing to do this.

The average person's attention online is currently 8.25 seconds (even goldfish have an average attention span of nine seconds)! Compare that to a habitual book reader who can concentrate for long periods. It takes about two minutes to read a single page in a book. Simply put, book buyers are your dream clients.

How do you find these fantastic, book reading dream clients? By writing a business book that 'calls out' to them.

You can use your book to zero in on exactly who you want in your audience, also known as your potential client pool. Perhaps you wish to work with people within a particular income bracket, or maybe you want to work with people with a certain mindset, background or belief?

Your book ought to deliberately set out to attract people you want, while also putting off people you don't want.

Case Study

Sarah, a corporate consultant, used a screening questionnaire to reduce the number of problematic clients she took on. However, she still found one too many clients with motivational problems that would slip through the net after several frustrating sessions.

Now, Sarah simply refuses to take on any new clients in her consultancy business without them first reading her book.

You don't need to be this strict for the results you want. By encouraging potential clients or new clients to read your book, you are testing their 'coachability' early on. This allows you to effortlessly remove those who will prove to be frustrating in the future.

Get Your Dream Clients to Refer You

Birds of a feather flock together. Incentivizing your dream clients to refer you to others is a powerful way to attract more dream clients.

Referrals are also powerful because they create a shortcut to the 'know, like and trust' factors we all need before we choose to work with someone. I bet you value what your friends, family and colleagues recommend, correct?

Most of us even value what strangers recommend. This is why Amazon has their review system. This is why there are many customer review sites, such as Trustpilot. People want 'social proof' that a company, product or service is worth their money. And we pay attention to these reviews, despite strangers writing them.

But when this social proof comes from friends or family, the impact can be astonishing. An entrepreneur friend of mine uses social proof from friends in a fantastic way. She's created a strategy where local businesses can encourage their customers to check in to their business on Facebook.

For example, a restaurant could offer a free dessert. Or a 10% discount on their meal. Or whatever offer they want to give.

By doing this, a local business gains a ton of exposure for their business. But it's not just any old exposure. People who see a friend checking into a business immediately think it's a recommendation from their friend.

This is far more powerful than a stranger's word, even if your friend never offers a review. Just seeing a friend check in is recommendation enough.

Every single business using this idea gains more customers and higher profits. This is the kind of money-can't-buy marketing that beats any flashy ad. When you see an ad, you think "I'm being sold to." But when a friend recommends something, it's not selling. They're doing you a favor. You know them, you like them and you trust their judgement.

Why Referrals are the Best Clients

Referrals are Pre-Sold to You and Your Products and Services

There's usually no need to sell to them. You are recommended by someone they value and trust. They validated you before they even walked through your door. All the typical cynicism is gone. Converting referrals into clients is a much smoother and pleasant process.

Referrals are Highly Unlikely to be Price Sensitive

If a good friend recommends a hairdresser, are you going to find out how much they charge and then look at other hairdressers in the area to compare? Of course not.

Someone you trust is giving you a valuable recommendation. So long as the cost isn't exorbitant, you'll go along with it. Referrals don't usually say things like, "I want to check out a few more places."

Referrals Become Higher-Quality Clients

As explained earlier, a current client referred them. So long as your business is attracting the kind of clients you want, then the referrals are likely to be cut from the same cloth.

Referrals are More Likely to Turn Into Long-Term Clients

In general, people are far more inclined to complain than recommend. So if someone is happy to recommend, referrals are likely to hold you at much higher regard and forge long-term relationships.

A Business Book as a Referral Tool

Anywhere between 10-20% of your clients will refer you to others. This minority loves to shout out to the world how wonderful you are. That still leaves a massive 80-90% who do not talk about you.

Why? Because many of us feel awkward doing anything that feels like selling. I know this because I'm terrible at referring people!

For example, I have a brilliant hairdresser. He's fantastic because I suffered from alopecia for many years, and he's the only hairdresser I know who really understands this. He has a way of cutting and coloring that gives my fine hair life and volume. As I write this, I'm looking at a stack of his business cards on my mantelpiece. Not one has ended up in the hands of my friends or family.

Of course, I'm always so happy to gush about him to anyone and everyone who compliments my hair, but it's so awkward to give out a business card! I did that once and was accused of being 'on commission.' That put me off so much I never tried again since.

Your clients also don't want to appear 'salesy.'

To get around this, many people use referral programs. These programs essentially bribe someone into referring you.

As one example, maybe you pay a one-off fee to a client who referred you to one of their friends. You could go one further and give them a percentage of the fees you charged the referral. This will reward clients who bring you the highest-paying referrals.

You could even reward your client on an ongoing basis. Maybe keep paying them a fee for as long as the referral uses your products or services. This entices them to refer people who will want to work with you on a long-term basis.

What do I think of referral programs? They have their place. I have one! However, I used the word 'bribe.' Since when did bribery have a good meaning? If you have to buy their attention, chances are their heart isn't really in it. If their heart isn't in it, then you're just someone they know.

What you really want is to be someone they love.

Plus, I see first-hand how people approach their new referral program while talking to clients. They're scared to talk about it because they have to 'sell the idea.'

Isn't that funny? The point of referral programs is so you can eliminate selling. This is a way for your clients to sell and find clients for you. And yet here you are forced into selling the referral program itself to your existing clients.

People don't like to sell. And they especially don't want to sell to their friends and family. It makes them feel uncomfortable. It begs the fear they will come across like some sort of salesperson for your business. Yes, you're offering them a monetary reward. But it's unlikely to be enough to override feelings of discomfort.

You know this, at least subconsciously, if not consciously.

This uncomfortableness makes it tricky for you to mention your referral program. *You're trying to bribe your clients into bribing their friends and family!*

Books, on the other hand, make it so easy for your current clients to refer you.

I'm not saying there isn't a place for a well-thought referral program, but in a head-to-head competition, books beat referral systems, hands down.

I can't say with any certainty why books are so much more powerful than referral systems, but I have at least one good theory: receiving a book is seen as a gift. Who doesn't like receiving gifts? In fact, who doesn't like giving gifts?

Gifts are fun for everyone, and books make awesomely fun gifts. So much fun, in fact, some cultures have holidays specifically for giving books.

The self-help industry was valued at $11.6 billion in 2019 and will grow to $13.2 billion by the end of 2022, according to MarketResearch.com. People are actively looking (and paying) for self-help or how-to books. People love gifts. People love books. People love self-help. Giving a self-help or how-to book is three luscious layers of awesome.

This is not lost on people who give books to others. Giving a book to a friend or family member makes you appear generous. Compare that to giving someone a business card. It's not even on the same page (pardon the pun).

Simply put, you wipe out any objections your clients may have about referring you when you give them your book as a referral tool.

Another theory why books do so much better than referral programs, is the fact people love to feel well-read or 'in the know.' This also includes an element of basking in reflected glory or what I call the Celebrity Halo. This is what makes people pull out their smartphone and beg a celebrity to take a selfie with them. And this is what makes them want to give a friend a book written by someone they know.

Giving away a book gives people intense feelings of satisfaction. They're not just helping a loved one. They're helping them with the perceived best in the business.

Also, with a book, you could opt not to give your clients any financial reward. All a successful referral will cost you is the price of a published book. You could make thousands ongoing from one referral, and it'll only ever cost you a book.

Case Study

Michael, a strategy consultant, had a referral program to encourage his clients to refer him. They got a finder's fee for every new referral that turned into a client.

After collaborating with me on a book, he scrapped the referral program altogether. Instead, he gives out several autographed copies of his book to each of his clients.

Despite his clients no longer receiving a finder's fee, his referrals are up by 55%.

I meet so many entrepreneurs who run themselves ragged doing a ton of marketing for their business. Instead, copy Michael and leverage your business book, then sit back and watch your own paying clients do all the marketing for you.

Referral Revenue Engine

Figure 1: Referral Revenue Engine

Step 1: Free Book Giveaway

The days of making millions from selling a business book are over. Now it's all about how you leverage a book.

One great way to leverage your book is by giving it away. Start with your favorite clients as they are your lowest hanging fruit.

Case Study

Aditya, a life coach, depended on referrals for 20% of her business. She wanted to increase this, but many of her clients were unwilling to refer her to their friends and family. They found it 'uncomfortable' despite being extremely happy with her services.

Her referrals grew by 65% after we developed her self-help book together. These days she is inundated with calls from her clients around the holidays because they want her book to give out to their friends and family as gifts.

Step 2: Forward Free Copies to Your Client's Network

What if your client receives the book to give away and then forgets about it? Offer to mail your book directly to their friends and colleagues and you increase your chances of referrals.

Step 3: Focus On Well-Connected Clients

You can make it even more pleasurable for well-connected clients to refer you by using personalization techniques. For example, say you're a business coach and one of your clients happens to be the CEO of a medium-sized firm, which means they of course know many other CEOs (birds of a feather, here again). For these people, you can make the process of referring you even sweeter, as the following case study proves.

Case Study

Michael, a strategy consultant, seeks permission to feature his favorite client in a special edition of his book. He then gives his client several copies and creates a pre-printed, personalized letter from his client that says, "I'm featured in this book and I'd love for you to have a copy."

You can imagine how thrilled his client is to be elevated from being a typical client. They are more than willing to reciprocate the favor by promoting the book to anyone they meet.

And Michael wins a lot more referrals.

Creating special editions of your book costs a little more than the other strategies here, but it can be well worth it for a well-connected client who can open doors for you.

> **Helpful Tip**
>
> If creating special editions of your book is either too costly or too difficult, just create the pre-printed, personalized letter.
>
> E.g. I got a lot from this book and thought you would too - <name of client>
>
> This alone will motivate others to give your book out.

Step 4: Feature Well-Connected Strategic Partners

Do you refer potential clients who are a bad fit for you to others and vice versa? Pinpoint anyone who seems to refer a lot of clients to you and provide them with free copies of your book. You allow them to generate goodwill from their clients with zero effort while they help you get referrals.

Just like with well-connected clients, these cross-referrers can also be further motivated. You can give these people pre-printed letters or special editions. You can 'sweeten the pot' further by offering them a referral fee if someone becomes your client.

Step 5: Flatter Well-Connected Service Providers

Many business owners hire other service providers with a lot of potential for referrals. For example, if you're a business coach helping new local businesses, you may refer clients to a great website designer. This designer will come into contact with lots of business owners who could benefit from your business coaching.

By providing free copies of your book, you make it extremely easy for them to refer clients to you. They become more valued in the eyes of their clients for giving them a useful resource, without any effort on their part. And, of course, any extra personalization that flatters them will motivate them to promote you even more.

Step 6: 'Franchise' Your Book

For your raving fans, you can take personalization to the max. It's incredibly cost-effective to create your book with a customized cover, all for them, thanks to print on demand. This works like gangbusters for clients, strategic partners and service providers alike.

Just imagine the previous example of the website designer. Do you think he'll refer clients to you when he can give them a professional, thought-provoking book? One that features his business and elevates his status in their eyes? Heck yeah!

> **Warning**
>
> When leveraged correctly, your book is a great referral tool.
>
> However, it's essential your book calls out to your dream clients, which will also dissuade those who are not a great fit for your business. The Referral Revenue Engine acts as a catalyst. If your book is angled toward your dream clients, you will generate the perfect referrals.
>
> However, if your book is general and appeals to anyone, you will attract all kinds of people and have to deal with clients who frustrate you.

Referrals on Autopilot

There's a reason why many people say that your fortune is in your network. Because it's true.

It'd be lovely to live in a world that was based purely on merit. But you and I know, success is usually about *who* you know more than what you can do.

This is why the Referral Revenue Engine is so important. The more you use it, the more you grow your book's reach (and therefore your reputation and authority). After a while, this will allow you to tap into the networks of key influencers.

At the top of your target market, there are people who don't need to sell themselves or their business at all.

They win referrals on autopilot.

Typically, referrals come from someone who is a current or former client. But when you're in the top flight, absolute strangers start referring to you. People who you don't know. People who certainly have never taken up your products or services or even walked through your doors. And yet, they take it upon themselves to talk positively about you.

This is the same reason your friend recommends the latest Leonardo DiCaprio movie. I doubt your friend has any personal relationship with DiCaprio. And yet here he is giving a glowing recommendation.

This kind of marketing feels like the stuff of dreams, and therefore unachievable. But it's well within your grasp when you have a business book.

You could go to endless networking meetings hoping to bump into the right people. Or use up every spare minute you have on the driving range, trying to increase your handicap. Hoping someone will invite you to some prestigious members club.

But, top-flight experts, influencers and entrepreneurs have one thing in common. They have a published book.

Writing a book is like getting a Willy Wonka Golden Ticket to the elite. Writing a book makes you a member of their club.

But it's not just about impressing the 'big guys' in your target market. Everyone puts books (and, by association, authors) on a pedestal. We teach children to prize books for their knowledge and wisdom.

We don't do this for most other types of written content.

Most of us automatically assume that someone who is well-read must be smart. Funny how that's never said about someone who's a TV addict.

In reality, depending on what programs they watch, a TV addict could be more knowledgeable than the book reader. And yet, the stereotype exists. As a business owner, you can leverage the value society places on books to enter the inner circles of influencers in your target market.

Many of my clients reach out to well-connected people by sending them a copy of their book. They are pleasantly surprised to find that these people see them as equals because they are a fellow author.

Fill Your Calendar with Dream Clients

As you know by now, using a book to do your marketing makes it so much easier to find your dream clients.

You'll find clients who are willing to digest a lot of information to find a solution, instead of those who become frustrated or lazy and then take it out on you.

You'll find your book will take on a new life as the ultimate referral tool. It makes it easy for people to refer new clients to you. It even makes it pleasurable for them to do so.

And finally, you'll attract clients who feel *designed* for you. Your book quickly weeds out all those who are unsuitable, leaving only your dream clients.

> ### Resource: Dream Client Worksheet
>
> If you only want to work with great clients, you need to become crystal clear on who they are. To help you identify them use the worksheet I've put together for you. Check the Resources section at the end of the book for all the download links or visit:
>
> - www.thefreedommasterplan.com/free-resources

This is only the beginning of what a business book can do for you and your business. Read on to discover how you can make more money consistently, within your business, without working harder.

In fact, you could work a lot less than you do now while increasing your profits.

CHAPTER 1: Quiz

Ready for your first quiz? Let's see how you get on. Remember, the answers are at the end of the book.

1. Define Celebrity Halo:
   - ☐ The need to become a celebrity at all costs
   - ☐ Creating fan fiction of your favorite celebrity
   - ☐ The urge to be associated with and bask in the reflected glory of a celebrity

2. Which is correct? You can leverage your business book to:
   - ☐ Find great coaches.
   - ☐ Find dream clients.
   - ☐ Find great software.

3. Which of these is *not* one of the steps inside the Referral Revenue Engine?
   - ☐ Free book giveaway
   - ☐ Price your book as high as you can.
   - ☐ Feature well-connected strategic partners.

CHAPTER 2

LEVERAGE YOUR BOOK TO INCREASE YOUR PROFITS

Would you like a better work-life balance? Isn't this why you left your day job? One way of cutting down your work hours is increasing your fees. But, I'm sure you know, that can be dangerous.

"How will my current clients feel? Will they ditch me and switch to a cheaper alternative? What about generating new clients? Will I lose out to a competitor?"

Due to these worries, many service-based business owners stay stuck in their current income bracket. And they're unwilling to make more money by working harder or longer hours than they already do.

Many go into business to take back control and choose the hours they work. And yet, the sad thing is, they're chained to the business, working harder (and longer) for themselves than they ever did for a boss.

In this chapter:

- you'll find two ways to earn more without working harder or longer in your business
- you'll discover how to multiply your current fees without experiencing resistance
- you'll find how easy it can be to build automated income streams that give you freedom to make money, even when you're not working
- and you'll get your hands on my Passive Income Assets Mind Map, a handy at-a-glance overview of how you can create these automated

income streams (I recommend you print and pin this up near your desk for daily inspiration)

Perception is Everything

There's a big secret about income that only a handful of people know at the top of their market. The more income you make, the more it is about *who* you are and not how good you are at a particular skill.

> *The more income you make, the more it is about* who *you are and not how good you are at a particular skill.*

It feels unfair, but it's true. This is important because so many business owners believe they need to *be* more to earn more. They need to have a few more years of experience, they need this or that qualification and so on.

They create all these reasons in their heads as to what they need to achieve so they can do more. And only when they can do more will they be able to charge more.

But this is not reality. Successful entrepreneurs are not paid more because they can do more. They don't always have more knowledge, skills, qualifications, education or experience.

So how do you achieve this 'who I am and not what I do' income level? By leveraging your business book to build unshakable authority.

Most people in the world will assume you are an authority on a subject if you've written a book on it. You're a fitness coach, and you've written a book on how middle-aged women can lose their muffin tops fast. Everyone assumes you must be an expert on this topic and have far more knowledge than other fitness coaches.

The way the world perceives you is key to how much you can charge for your products, programs or services. The higher your perceived authority, the more you can charge, without complaints.

Authors Command Authority

It's not a coincidence that the word 'author' is inside the word 'authority.' Both terms come from the same French word 'auctor.' The world expects someone who has authority to demonstrate their authority by becoming an author.

Because of this, the vast majority of people in the world see authorship as a one-way street. You gain authority first through hard work. Then you become an author. Cause and effect.

So yes, you can write a book because you're an authority on a subject. But the reverse is also true. You can *become* an authority simply because you've written a book. Why wait for authority when you can create authority for yourself?

Your book is the perfect tool to build your authority and position you as an expert in your field. Nearly every business owner has a website, business cards, sales pages, brochures, etc. But how many are published authors?

> Why wait for authority when you can create authority for yourself?

By virtue of having a published book, you are elevated and differentiated from others in your field. You're not one of many. *You're in a different league.*

You're no longer an executive coach, for example. You're *the* executive coach who is an authority on leadership skills because you wrote a book on it.

Never shy away from mentioning your book in all your interactions. This is not the time to be coy. Many of my former book clients are now minor celebrities in their field. All because they proudly mention they are published authors wherever they go.

Case Study

Liz is a fitness coach. The book we wrote together opened up the doors to speaking engagements. But she wasn't happy to wait for success to slowly develop. She wanted unshakeable authority fast.

Liz holds book signings after her speeches. Her assistants manufacture them so they look and feel like the book signings of top novelists. People line up and have their books autographed by her. They even have pictures taken with her.

This strategy has really sped up her authority journey.

Within months she was interviewed several times on radio and even on local TV. Not only that, the authority she manufactured was now attracting other authorities, keen to collaborate, which boosted her authority even further.

Liz is now a bona fide authority, which allows her to charge several times the fees of most other fitness coaches.

Warning

Do not focus on book sales.

Liz was not focused on book sales. She usually gives her book away by including it in the goody bags for event attendees.

Her focus is on using her book to shortcut her way to authority.

The book helps her create an army of fans who act like a talented sales force, without needing a salary.

Helpful Tip

Another way to accelerate your authority status is to collaborate with other authorities.

Liz's book has been reprinted twice, each time with an introduction or guest chapter from another authority figure.

Also, these books have new covers with endorsement blurbs from various other authorities.

Both of these increase her authority by association.

Additionally, she counter-endorses other people's books, exposing her to thousands of new potential clients.

Case Study

Michael, a strategy consultant, was asked to speak at a seminar held by a large bank because his book was discovered by the head of HR. The beautiful thing about having a book you are proud to promote is that you never know whose hands it might fall into next.

Michael discovered the CEO was attending the seminar. Michael asks to meet the CEO after his speech. The CEO is so impressed with Michael's speech, he asks Michael to create a full program to roll out to all UK branches.

This was something Michael never imagined. Up until this point, he worked for small to medium-sized businesses. Now he is creating a program for a national bank.

Of course, as he's my friend, I'm likely to be biased and say he is an exceptional consultant. But I'm sure there are other consultants just as good and, dare I say, better than Michael. And yet, here he is, getting the respect of being the best, as well as a handsome six-figure contract.

> ## Case Study
>
> Sarah, a corporate consultant, leverages her book wherever she goes. This attracts the attention of a website building company because she recommends their software in her book.
>
> Of course, it made sense for this company to approach her and ask her to become their (very well-paid) spokesperson.

These are a few examples from my former clients. Once you get out there and fearlessly leverage your book, it will appear that money hunts you down.

Liz, Michael and Sarah achieved their successes because they were proud of their books. They were proud to promote it at every opportunity. Each of them is an authority because they *decided* to become an authority. No one gave them permission. They chose it.

I meet so many entrepreneurs who are waiting for permission to be an authority. This permission can be in the form of qualifications, a certain number of years in business, a certain level of profits or some other excuse,

The truth is, only you can give yourself permission.

So, if you've written a book, you have permission to get out there and tell everyone about it. And if you have no book yet, please give yourself a break and stop waiting for permission. You have now discovered the art of reverse engineering.

You don't need to be an authority to write a book. Instead, you can write a book to *get* authority. This authority allows you to be seen head and shoulders above your competition, so you can dictate your prices.

> ## Helpful Tip
>
> Use your book as a powerful replacement for business cards. You'll stand out from the crowd. After each networking meeting, I bet you go home with a pocketful of business cards. Do you struggle to remember who gave you which card? Would you remember who gave you a valuable book? Yes, you would!

Case Study

Aditya, a life coach, recently told me that she no longer carries business cards. Instead, she keeps copies of her book in her purse whenever she's at conferences, events and networking meetings.

Every time, people she meets readily take all of her books. Many others are disappointed that they 'missed out' and want details of the book so they can order it online.

Can you imagine this with business cards? I think not.

Business cards belong in that bag of tricks called selling. Along with brochures, leaflets, sales pages, landing pages and anything else that screams 'buy me!'

Books, on the other hand, are sources of expert information that are valued and even chased after. Also, in a big networking event where everyone goes home with a stack of business cards, who stays top of mind? The author who gave you a book, of course!

Furthermore, Aditya tells me she carries at least one copy of her book wherever she goes.

She explains that you never know where there might be an opportunity. Indeed she's had strangers strike up conversations on planes, trains and department stores.

When the conversation moves to, "So, what do you do" she's ready with her book. "Oh, I won't bore you with the typical elevator pitch. Let me give you this." On cue, she excuses herself to the restroom and lets the book work its magic.

Usually, she gets a call within weeks for coaching, to speak at functions, requests for interviews, etc.

Earning Money While You Sleep

So far we've looked at how you can make more money by increasing your fees without fear of losing business. Leveraging the authority you build as a published author allows you to free yourself from competing with others and getting into 'price wars.'

However, there are only so many hours in the day for you to work. When you sell knowledge or skills by the hour, there is always a cap as to how much you can earn.

The idea of making money without working, or making money while you sleep, sounds spammy. Like those awful 'biz opp' adverts. Just press this button and wait to be smacked in the face with wads of cash. And yet, there is an element of truth.

It *is* possible to earn while you sleep. So long as you're willing to invest some time, effort and money at the beginning.

For example, if you own property that you rent out, you are making money while you sleep. Yes, there are little maintenance jobs here and there. But after the initial investments of money, time and effort, it becomes an asset. It continues to make money for you without you doing much in return.

Compare that to how many service-based entrepreneurs work in their businesses. They charge fees, either on an hourly, project or event basis. They barter their time for money. They exchange knowledge for cash. As soon as this exchange stops, the money stops. Even if you're an authority that charges far more than others, you are not earning when you are sleeping.

A business coach and friend of mine drilled into me the difference between entrepreneurs and the self-employed. You might think they mean the same thing, but I promise you, they don't. Many people fall into the trap of thinking they're an entrepreneur, when in fact they are self-employed. Just because you're the boss, this does not make you an entrepreneur.

For example, a fitness coach who works for himself is not an entrepreneur. He is self-employed. He's no different from a coach employed by a large health club. The only difference is he will need to find clients himself.

The self-employed struggle to become wealthy because they are only paid so long as they are working. They sell knowledge by the hour. They exchange their skills and time for money. And as soon as they stop, their earnings stop.

This is the reality for many service-based business owners. By striking out on their own, all they've done is give themselves a job. To add insult to injury, they now need to spend time doing activities they dislike, such as marketing, selling and lead generation.

I met many people who worked for corporations, but they wanted the freedom of being their own boss. They decide to become an entrepreneur and 'go it alone.' They end up devoting more of their time to lead generation and selling. And less time doing what they love (making a difference through their work).

Even once successful, with a calendar full of loyal clients, they're still bartering skills and time for money. If you earn solely from selling knowledge by the hour, eventually you'll hit a glass ceiling where you physically can't make any more money. Not only that, you'll need to put in the same time and effort every day to stay at the same profitability level.

This is the reality of the self-employed.

Let's compare this to an entrepreneur. Entrepreneurs choose to hold assets that they create once and get paid for again and again passively. This is like a property owner who leases his property to a tenant.

There are many ways of creating these assets. But, without a doubt, the fastest way is through a business book. If you're a published author, you can use your book as a base to develop products and services that become what I call Passive Income Assets.

These will allow you to earn an income, even while sleeping.

What's fantastic with these 'extra' revenue streams is that most only need a little bit of effort in the beginning to get started. Then they run on their own, making extra profits (and sometimes more than your main income).

Let's look at a few ideas.

Passive Income Assets

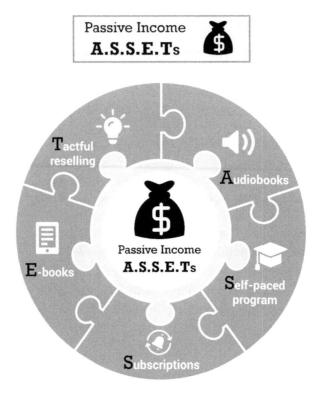

Figure 2: Passive Income A.S.S.E.Ts

Audiobooks

For many authors, this is the first and easiest money-making Passive Income Asset.

Many people who dislike reading enjoy audiobooks. That means you can earn the attention of potential clients who would never find you otherwise.

Audiobooks allow people to 'read' on the go. You can reach the busiest of people who don't have time to read a book. People also expect to pay two to three times more for an audiobook than a paperback book, which allows you to generate more income.

> **Warning**
>
> Do not attempt a homemade recording using amateur equipment, such as your smartphone.
>
> Homemade recordings sound terrible. If you've ever tried to record your voice, you'll understand why.
>
> I'm always amazed at how a microphone can pick up the tiniest of throat clicks and spit sounds. And don't get me started on breathing noises!
>
> Keep in mind that your audiobook represents you and your business. Your target clients expect a professional recording.

I advise that you choose either to hire a professional recording studio or buy professional recording equipment.

A professional studio will allocate you an audio producer who will remove all these extra sounds that magically turn up in home recordings. They can also add music and sound effects if necessary. And they will use the best technology that suits the main music formats, such as MP3s.

The other option is recording yourself. This may appear as the cheaper option, but it is not. You need to invest in professional recording and editing software. And you will need a professional-grade microphone and headset. None of this comes cheap.

Don't scrimp on this equipment. You're creating an asset that will continue to pay you for years to come. This is a small price to pay for a professional product that can turn into a lucrative passive income stream.

You also need to factor in the downtime spent learning how to use the software. Remember, time is money. Honestly, I would only recommend recording yourself if you have experience in this field. Otherwise, it's best to leave it to the professionals.

There is a 'halfway' option. Audio producers can advise you on buying a professional microphone to record yourself at home. Then you send the recording to them to finish it to a professional level.

This option is the perfect solution for anyone who cannot afford to devote one to two days for studio sessions or does not have the means to travel to a studio.

Helpful Tip

Regarding whether to use a professional voiceover artist or not is up to you. If you feel you have a great recording voice, go for it.

The benefit of this is you save money. You're also able to show off your personality and connect with your listeners.

On the other hand, some voices don't sound great on a recording.

If you're unsure, ask a close friend or family member who is known to be brutally honest.

Self-Paced Programs

This Passive Income Asset takes a little more time and effort than producing an audiobook. However, the upside is that it has the potential to pay you back far more in profit.

You may charge perhaps two to three times more for an audiobook compared to a paperback.

But you could charge at least ten times the cost of your book for a self-paced program. I know people charging up to fifty times the cost of their book.

A typical program will have some or all of the following:

- DVDs, MP4s or equivalent
- CDs, MP3s or equivalent
- forms
- templates
- workbooks

- cheat sheets
- access to special student-only websites
- access to student-only webinars or teleseminars
- recordings of seminars
- recordings of consultations

It's easy to offer most of this online in a digital format, which is a lot cheaper than sending out items in the post. You could even have an online university with different courses. This allows you to seriously cut down on delivery costs.

Helpful Tip

I advise you to keep one or two elements as physical items instead of all digital.

I understand why you would want to digitize everything because of the low costs. However, sending some physical items out in the post helps keep customers happy.

I know one successful marketer who sends his workbooks in the mail. Everything else in his course is digitized. Sending out just one physical item reduces his refund rates by around 30%.

Now you might think that creating a self-paced program sounds like a lot of work. This couldn't be further from the truth. You'll find most items are either already in your business or very easily created with a little imagination.

Around six months after publishing his book, Sean, a marketing consultant, decided to put together a program. Let's look at how he did this with minimal effort.

Case Study

Within a couple of months of publishing his book, Sean turned it into a digital audiobook. I explained earlier how this is the easiest Passive Income Asset to create. He did just that.

Several months later, when creating his self-paced program, the audiobook was there waiting to be included. The only extra thing he did was send it to a specialist company who converted it into a CD series. This is not a mandatory step. Sean has an older audience who still value physical CDs. You don't have to do this if your audience prefers a digital audiobook.

Next, he was asked to speak at several seminars and conferences. This was mainly because of the authority he gained from being a published author.

The event organizers recorded many of these events. They were happy to give him a copy of his speech. Again, no extra work was required to include these in his program.

As explained previously, Sean has an older audience. So he chose to spend a little money to have these speeches converted into DVDs. This is a step you don't have to take if your audience would be happy with a digital recording.

Helpful Tip

The great thing about live recordings is that people are more forgiving, when it comes to sounds, than with audiobooks. Sounds such as clicks, microphone feedback, etc., are expected. There's no need to have them polished by a professional in a studio.

However, if the organizer is not recording your speech, seek a professional with the correct recording equipment.

Your audience may forgive the sound quality of live speeches. But they won't forgive a speech that looks to be recorded on an iPhone.

Remember, your products represent you and your business.

Case Study *(continued)*

Next, Sean decided to have a look at what he provides his current consultancy clients.

During a consultation, I explained how he could re-position many items he already has. Sean found a plethora of templates, forms, workbooks, checklists and other paraphernalia he uses for his current clients that are perfect for inclusion in his program.

Yes, they needed a little tweaking here and there to fit, but this took only a few hours of his time.

Lastly, he wanted to add items that would pump up the value, so he could charge a premium for his program.

He added a live one-hour webinar at the end of each month. This allowed new customers who had bought his program the chance to ask questions. He also offered a one-to-one 15-minute consultation.

These two items were the only items he added to his program that took a little time and effort to fulfil.

When Sean first thought of creating a self-paced program, he assumed it would take weeks, if not months, to create. And yet, he managed to put the bulk of his program together within days.

Creating a self-paced program is simpler than you think.

If you don't like doing webinars, or you don't want to do consultations like Sean, you don't have to. Adding a live element and some personalization allows you to charge more for your program. But they are not necessary.

However, if you do add these elements, you'll find a hidden benefit. These elements allow you to make more money. Let's got back to Sean to see how he does this.

Case Study

Sean holds his one-hour webinar mainly so new self-paced program students can ask questions. But they also build a connection with him. Many of these students want more regular interaction.

This allows him to create another lucrative Passive Income Asset, a monthly membership program (a type of subscription - more on this later). He uses the live webinar to sell this monthly membership program, with great success.

At the end of the live webinar, he casually asks if anybody needs regular support. He then mentions his monthly membership program with a deep loyalty discount for self-paced program students.

On average, 25% of his students progress to his monthly membership program. This earns him a long-term income. It's the same with his one-to-one 15-minute consultations. He uses his one-to-one sessions to give each student clarity on his program. However, depending on their needs, he may also mention his monthly membership program. Or if he feels they are suitable (and have the financial capacity), he may mention his one-to-one consulting.

Plus, he keeps the consultations down to 15 minutes. This means that students not suitable for upgrades can still receive clarity, without taking up too much of his time.

What you wish to include in your self-paced program is entirely up to you.

Fearful of doing speeches and therefore have no recordings? No problem. Perhaps you created some instructional videos for clients. Include those in the program. Have you been podcasting or maybe interviewed for someone else's podcast? Include those recordings.

Add whatever makes you feel comfortable. The best advice I can give you, when starting out, is start small.

As you found out in the previous case study, Sean's program has a lot of 'moving parts' which is why he charges $800 for it. You don't have to go all out as he did straight away. You can create a much simpler self-paced program.

For example, a program consisting of an audio recording of your book, a workbook, a few templates, forms and other materials you currently use within your business.

Also, add in a copy of your book. Yes, there's a chance that your would-be student has a copy, but they may not. People value books. Even if they have a copy, there's a good chance they may give the second book to a friend. This means more exposure for you.

A simple program like this could sell for $97 or more. Compare that to the average of $5-15 for a paperback or hardback book. This is six to ten times the revenue.

As you win more exposure, you can add more items as you go along. This allows you to increase the price of your program accordingly.

Subscriptions

This Passive Income Asset can create the most profitable income streams.

With most other Passive Income Assets, such as audiobooks and self-paced programs, you earn a one-off payment. With subscriptions, a customer can pay you for *years*.

One type of subscription is monthly membership programs that give students ongoing support. They can include:

- regular webinars or teleseminars
- dedicated website or directory
- regular e-mails and newsletters
- forums and networking opportunities between members

Helpful Tip

I advised this before with self-paced programs. It's the same for monthly membership programs. An excellent idea is to have one tangible item sent in the mail, instead of digitizing the whole program. This could reduce your refund rates by up to 30%.

To keep costs down, why not choose something cheap to send, such as a printed monthly newsletter?

Your customers will value getting something 'real' every month, along with all the digital goodies.

Remember, monthly membership programs are also great places to find higher-ticket clients.

You found out earlier that some of Sean's self-paced program students wanted to upgrade to his monthly membership program. In the same way, you'll find some of your membership students will upgrade to your higher-level offerings.

That's the beauty of creating these Passive Income Assets. You're creating residual income streams. You're not relying solely on selling knowledge or skills by the hour. But they also join forces to promote your other products, programs and services.

Some people may go straight from reading your book to becoming a high-ticket client. But most people will need more 'wooing.'

Adding Passive Income Assets, such as audiobooks, self-paced programs and subscriptions, allows this to happen. They work together to solidify your status as an expert and authority that started from your book. And this of course means more dream clients.

Another type of subscription is done-for-you services. For example, say you coach new business owners. You could offer done-for-you website design and hosting. Or perhaps done-for-you newsletters or e-mails for these business owners to send to their customers. You could offer done-for-you social media marketing or done-for-you search engine optimization.

Don't worry, you don't have to offer these services yourself or know much about them. This is the perfect time to find partners to provide these services. Not only does this add a lucrative residual income, you'll also find your new partner may be able to cross-refer clients.

E-books

This is less of a money-spinner and more of an extension of having a published book. The profits are in the larger audience you reach.

E-book readers have soared in popularity over the last decade. You must include them in your marketing plan. Many people don't even buy physical books anymore, choosing the convenience of e-books. Which means you could be missing out on a ton of potential clients if you overlook this. Therefore, you should make sure your book is available, at the very least, on Amazon Kindle.

Depending on your target market, you could also publish on Apple iBooks, Google Play Books, Nook, and Kobo.

Warning

Do not publish *only* to e-book format. Your book should also be available in paperback format.

I've seen many people publish only in e-book format. This doesn't earn the authority of a 'real' book. People see e-books everywhere now. They visit websites every day asking them to leave their e-mail address in exchange for an e-book. Because of this, the power of e-books is greatly reduced.

The trick is to have a paperback version along with the digital format. This gets that authority you want, without losing people who prefer to consume your book digitally.

Tactful Reselling

The last Passive Income Asset is for those of you further along in your asset creation journey. If you're only starting, I advise you to tuck this idea away for a few months.

This idea is different from the others as it's not about *building* a Passive Income Asset. This is about using your *existing* Passive Income Assets in a smart way.

You could choose to sell your assets to other people tactfully. One way of doing this is licensing, where you allow another business owner to resell your Passive Income Assets. For example, you could license out your self-paced program.

You might think, "Why would I do that? Wouldn't that be helping my competition?"

Not if you license to a specific location. In large countries, such as the USA, you could license to a different state from where you operate. Then there would be no competition issues. In smaller countries, you can choose to license to another country altogether. This allows you to monetize your Passive Income Assets further.

Not only that, when somebody buys a geographical license from you, your name is still on these assets. Think about this for a second. Someone else will build your reputation and brand for you in a different area of the country. Or maybe even an entirely different country altogether. And they pay you for the privilege!

I've heard of entrepreneurs generating new clients and speaking opportunities halfway across the world because of licensing.

Private label is similar to licensing but takes it one step further. When someone buys a private label, they want to pass off your Passive Income Asset as their own.

The downside of this is you don't have the benefits of other people building your brand.

The upside? I see entrepreneurs charge up to 50X the cost of a geographical license for a private label license. Offering a private label license is a great way to make a lot of money upfront for a Passive Income Asset.

This is a fantastic idea if the person buying it is in a region of the world where you have no interest in building your brand.

Resource: Passive Income Assets Mind Map

To help you, I've created a handy, at-a-glance mind map that shows you all the different income assets.

Make sure you print this out and hang up near your place of work.

This will keep you motivated in building these profitable residual income streams. Check out the Resources section near the back of the book for the link.

Earn More Without Working Harder

When you are proud of your book, and take every opportunity to promote it, you build authority. This authority elevates you from your competition to the point where you are perceived as the expert, allowing you to increase your fees. Not only that, you can use your book to build an empire of Passive Income Assets.

These assets produce secondary income streams that operate separately from your 'main' business. They allow you to take time out of your business without seeing your income dry up entirely.

Don't be shy. Taking pride in your book will allow you to increase your profits without working harder or longer.

Resource: Take Your First Step With Me

Unsure of your first step? I've given you a lot of different Passive Income Assets in this chapter. If you're feeling a little bewildered at where to start, I'd love to help you create a clear passive income strategy.

See the 'Need More Help?' section for how to book a consultation with me or e-mail:

- mitali@thefreedommasterplan.com

In the next chapter, you're going to discover how you can leverage your book to eliminate panic-inducing sales calls (my number one fear).

Chapter 2: Quiz

1. The more income you make, the more it is about…
   - ☐ How good you are at a particular skill.
   - ☐ Who you are and not how good you are at a particular skill.
   - ☐ How many qualifications you have.

2. Which two below are Passive Income Assets?
   - ☐ Self-paced program.
   - ☐ Subscription.
   - ☐ Speaking engagement.

3. What are the two types of subscriptions?
   - ☐ Audiobooks and self-paced programs.
   - ☐ E-books and audiobooks.
   - ☐ Monthly membership programs and done-for-you services.

CHAPTER 3

LEVERAGE YOUR BOOK TO REMOVE SALES ANXIETY

Many years ago, as a teenager, I landed my first part-time telephone sales job for a well-known window insulation firm in the UK.

My very simple job is calling members of the public, at dinner time of course, and convincing them to let our friendly sales representatives inside their home. Easy, right? Except, there is no basic salary. My wages are 100% commission. In other words, if I don't sell, I don't earn. I don't earn, I don't eat.

This is so terrifying. I still remember my hands trembling while I listened to the dial tone. I remember how my voice would sound unusually high as I read the sales script. I remember the beads of sweat dripping down the back of my neck, staining my favorite blouse, as I got to the 'close' part of the call. This job is my idea of a living nightmare.

As I'm sure you guessed, I didn't last long. Five days to be exact.

Yes, this is an extreme example. I am cold calling members of the public who had no prior interest in window insulation. In most selling situations, the potential client has at least shown some interest. Perhaps they're responding to an ad. Or they walked into a place of business. This was not the case here.

I think back now and wonder how the job would have felt if I offered people a book instead. One that explained how much money they would save on heating costs with energy-efficient double glazing. It would have been a walk in the park!

Promoting a product or service is nerve-wracking because you are selling. Promoting a book is easy because you are no longer selling. You're giving the gift of information.

In this chapter:

- you'll learn why your book is the best sales tool you will ever possess
- and you'll discover some simple strategies you can use to leverage your book to do all the selling for you

Implement these, and you will have permanent freedom from sales anxiety.

Salesperson vs Expert

If you could invite anyone to dinner, dead or alive, who would your guest be?

You might say Mahatma Gandhi. Or Bob Proctor, John Lennon, Barack Obama or any number of amazing people. But my guess is that you wouldn't pick Grant Cardone, Jordan Belfort or any other well-known salesperson.

Chances are, your choice will be an expert of some sort. Not to say salespeople are not experts at sales and social sciences, we seem to favor experts. Whether in the field of science, film, music or whatever category.

Most of us have become extremely wary of salespeople after decades of door-to-door sales and cold calls. We don't like salespeople because, in traditional sales, there's always been one winner and one loser.

If the salesperson gets the deal, they are the winner. The customer is the loser. If the customer can resist, he is the winner and the salesperson the loser. This is a dirty game of words and wills where each party is trying to outwit the other. No wonder most of us think of sales as sleazy or manipulative.

The sad thing is, this is not true of every salesperson. There are people out there who sell in such a way that it's a beautiful experience. Beautiful for both the seller and the buyer. It's true what they say. We don't like being sold to, but we love to buy.

> Salespeople are like toupees or wigs. You only notice the bad ones!

We come across these wonderful salespeople all the time. But sadly, we tend to remember the terrible, pushy salespeople. Salespeople are like toupees or wigs. You only notice the bad ones!

Natural, pressure-free selling is an incredible skill and one that you can learn. But it takes time and effort.

I'm sure you've heard of the 10,000-hour rule. This is talked about in many well-known books for several years. Books such as Geoff Colvin's Talent is Overrated, Malcolm Gladwell's Outliers, and The Talent Code by Daniel Coyle.

The basic premise is that you need to put in 10,000 hours into learning any skill to be an expert. Even if you're terrible at something, if you put in around 10,000 hours, you'll be great at it.

This gave me an entirely new way of looking at myself. I realized that when I told people I wasn't good at something, that's not what I truly meant. Subconsciously what I meant to say was, "I'm *not willing* to spend time and effort getting good at this."

Sales is a great skill. And if you're willing to put in the time and effort, you can become very good at it. This is especially true if you learn the natural, pressure-free type of sales, not the sleazy, pushy version.

But I don't want to spend time and effort in learning sales. I respect people who do. But I'd rather spend my time doing things I love, such as honing my writing skills or mentoring my students.

Many business owners are the same. They are technicians. They have this unique skill of transforming people and solving their problems. This is their main focus. They didn't expect that, to be successful, they needed to learn how to sell.

This is one of the key reasons many highly-skilled people never receive the recognition or level of earnings they deserve. In contrast, modestly-skilled people may do well simply because they are great salespeople.

Now let's contrast this with an expert. An expert is someone you'd never expect to appear at your door. Or call you out of the blue. With most experts, you can't turn up at their office or call them up and get straight through.

When you think of a salesperson, you immediately think of glossy brochures, flashy PowerPoint presentations or other sales material. All ready to lure you into the sale.

When you think of an expert, you think of peer-reviewed research papers. Or cuttings from newspaper and magazine articles. Videos and audios of interviews. And yes, you guessed it, books.

Who would you choose to invite to dinner; the salesperson who potentially could make things uncomfortable by trying to sell to you, or the expert who can entertain you and others with their knowledge and expertise?

The irony is that experts are the best salespeople. They outsell a salesperson at every opportunity. If you look at top experts in any field, they're making an incredibly comfortable income from selling. They're selling themselves and their skills.

Famous singers and actors are great at promoting their albums and films. Even political and spiritual leaders are selling. They sell their ideas. And yet, these experts never appear to be selling anything.

I said this in the previous chapter, but it's worth repeating. The assumption is that you must be an expert or an authority to have a published book. But now you know the reverse is also true. You can attain expert status and authority by writing a book.

Earlier you discovered how a book completely bypasses selling. Brochures, leaflets, fliers, print adverts, sales pages, radio ads, TV ads, etc., are all viewed as marketing materials. Their purpose is to make a sale. A book is a source of expert information that is to be valued.

Because of this, fear and anxiety evaporate when you switch from promoting *you* to promoting *your book*. Promoting yourself feels 'salesy' while promoting a book feels revealing and enlightening. I've seen entrepreneurs who were terrible at promoting themselves transform into calm and collected professionals. All because they moved the focus off them and on to their books.

There's a belief in us that, when someone promotes a book, they're *giving* you the gift of education. When someone promotes their products or services, they are *asking* you for money (selling).

Helpful Tip

A 'catalyst' to grabbing attention is offering a book that has an award.

If you hit bestseller status on Amazon, make sure you state this on your book cover. However, depending on the topic of your book, getting bestseller status may not be easy.

Another way to get attention and authority is to win an award. Just one award allows you to display 'award-winning' on your book cover.

A great place to start is:

- www.awards-list.com/international-business-awards

This site has a comprehensive list of award-giving organizations and how to apply for them. Yes, it may take some effort with the application process. But the attention from being able to use the award on your book cover is well worth it

Another way is to be cited in magazines, newspapers, radio and TV. More on that later.

Diagnostic Selling

In your business, do you sell or do you diagnose? Let me explain.

Several years ago, I was referred to a maxillofacial surgeon after cracking my jaw in three different places. Thankfully, he informed me I could avoid facial surgery as long as I did not chew for three months. However, if he felt I needed operating on immediately, chances are I would have agreed.

Now let's say my family doctor diagnosed me with a broken jaw and told me he wished to operate on me.

I probably would have demanded a second opinion.

Why? Because my family doctor is a generalist. He's not an expert and an authority on facial reconstructive surgery.

After watching many business owners, I discovered they are the same. They also fall into either the expert or generalist category. And this dictates whether they are forced to sell. Or whether they have a much more comfortable life using what I call Diagnostic Selling.

Because, when you are seen by others as an expert in your field, you never have to sell.

Michael, a strategy consultant, demonstrates this well.

Case Study

Because of the authority he gained from publishing and leveraging his book, Michael diagnoses instead of selling.

Typically, a potential client contacts him because they either read his book or a current client has referred them. The potential client is guided to an online questionnaire where they answer questions about their business, their needs and challenges, and why they want to work with him. They are then led to his appointment booking system to book an initial call.

So far, so normal. But here's the rub. The potential client has to pay $197 for the call. Yes, Michael charges for the call.

This transforms the call from a sales call to a genuine consultation. No one would pay for a sales call, but they do for a consultation.

Before the call, he arranges for the potential client to receive a copy of his book (if necessary). In the questionnaire, he instructs the potential client to read his book in preparation for the call. No preparation will mean the call is pointless, and he will give no refunds. The potential client risks wasting $197.

On the call, Michael listens briefly to the potential client's needs. Bear in mind, the questionnaire gives him an accurate picture. He is able to quickly diagnose the potential client's problems and offer his solutions by the end of the 30-minute call.

In the last five years, only eleven of these potential clients did not take up his services after diagnosis. Oh, and as a side note, his ongoing consulting fees are around five to ten times the market average. And yet he never has to sell a thing.

This is the power of authority. The power of an expert.

Now, let's compare that to a typical service-based business owner. A potential client finds their details online. The potential client looks around the website to see if this person could help them. They fill out a contact form, send an e-mail or book in for a (free) sales call.

This is never called a sales call, of course. The word sales makes most people apprehensive. So it's called something else, such as strategy call, clarity call or discovery call. Whatever it takes to not scare the potential client away. In the meantime, the potential client looks at other similar providers in the area.

On the sales call, the potential client takes up most of the time explaining their needs. Toward the end, the business owner explains a little bit about what they can do and then makes an offer (i.e., selling).

How this usually ends is the potential client wanting time to 'think it over.' What this means is they want to speak to a few other providers and make a price comparison.

Can you see the difference?

First, as an expert and an authority, you can charge for things that others give away for free, such as the initial call (if this fits your business model).

Second, you move from a position of selling to diagnosing, where the sale is almost assumed. This is even more potent when someone has paid for the call, as they're now a buyer. But this strategy works even with free consultations.

Michael never has to lower himself to 'selling.' He is an expert and an authority. All he does is diagnose problems and offer solutions.

Lastly, you are elevated above price comparisons. You're not just another coach, consultant, designer, accountant, etc. You are the coach, consultant, etc., who wrote that book. You become incomparable to a 'standard' business owner in the same niche.

When you take the opportunity to promote your book at every opportunity, it becomes your salesperson. You no longer have to sell.

Remember, no one wants to invite a salesperson to dinner. But they'd happily invite an interesting expert author. Others see you as an expert and not a salesperson. You let your book do the selling.

Zero Selling System

A minority of your book readers will resonate with your book so much, they will sign up to work with you almost immediately. However the majority will not. Most people need a little bit more wooing. That's when you can use what I call the Zero Selling System.

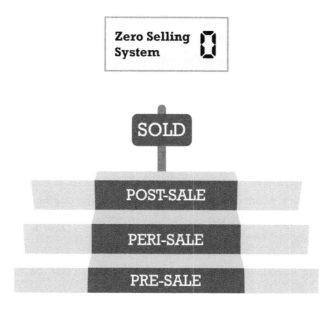

Figure 3: Zero Selling System

The sales process of most businesses goes through three phases, which are:

- pre-sale
- peri-sale (during the sale)
- post-sale

As the name suggests, pre-sale is the nerve-wracking, sweat-inducing phase of sales that most of us hate. I just discussed Diagnostic Selling which demonstrates how a book eliminates these pre-sale issues.

What's interesting and reassuring to those who dislike sales is that a book also supports us in the later selling phases.

An example of peri-sale would be a potential client who has booked you for an initial call. They are very interested in you and your products or services as they have read your book. But you need to 'tip them over the edge' in the call and convert them into a client. Many authors have discovered that quoting individual sections of their book is persuasive, without feeling 'salesy.'

This reminds me of being in church, listening to a priest back up his teachings by quoting sections of the Bible. In the same way, quoting sections of your book eliminates the need to sell yourself on the call. There is no need to be pushy. You listen to their needs and then point to sections of your own book to 'back up' your diagnosis.

Your diagnosis, of course, is that they need your products or services.

The final phase is the post-sale phase. Many business owners forget about this, to their detriment. You now know that your book is the best sales tool you will ever have. More people will choose to become paying clients through your book than practically any other sales materials. However, nobody has a 100% close rate.

Aditya, a life coach, explained to me how she attracts back these 'lost' prospects.

Case Study

When a new prospect doesn't become a client, Aditya starts making a care package. She highlights relevant pages using sticky notes and mails the book to them.

She reports that she gets around 50% of these lost prospects back.

Helpful Tip

Aditya also gifts special versions of her book to different clients.

She sends an autographed copy of her book to all new clients. And she sends a beautifully bound hardcover version on the anniversary of them working together.

As you can imagine, this turns them into super fans who want to continue their relationship with her for years.

In-Person Selling

Even in a world full of technology, there is still sometimes the need to sell or promote yourself in person, especially at your place of work.

Being on your home turf is the number one way to remove sales anxiety because you are, by nature 'at home.' However, there's a lot more to making a great first impression than your outfit in these situations.

They say you shouldn't judge a book by its cover, but everyone does (pardon the pun).

Harry, a financial consultant, knows that first impressions are everything. He creates an office environment that evokes authority, credibility and respect.

Let's go through, step by step, how he does this.

Step 1: Display Your Book Prominently

You discovered earlier the elevated perception of books in comparison to most other forms of written content. We create bookshelves and cases to display them in. We build libraries to house them in to be shared with our community. Use this to your advantage.

> ### Case Study
>
> Harry displays his book prominently on an ornate bookcase behind his desk and chair. He positions several copies of his book with other renowned authors in his field, benefiting from the reflected glory.
>
> Nearly every new prospect is impressed and can't help but ask him about his book.

Warning

Don't have books that look like you've never opened them. People usually know when someone is trying to manufacture the air of authority.

Instead, use books that you have read within your industry.

As an entrepreneur, chances are you do a lot of reading. Don't hide those books away. Fetch them out of the attic or wherever you stored them. Dust them off and place them on your bookshelf. The more thumbed and 'used' they look, the better. You could add sticky notes to mark individual pages.

The impression you want to give is 'educated, knowledgeable and informed.' That never happens with books looking just-delivered from Amazon.

Step 2: Have Copies in Your Waiting Room or Reception Area

Harry leaves a couple of copies on the table in his waiting room. Even if someone is making a quick visit and not entering his office, he is still able to make an impression.

Not only that, some clients come with partners or friends.

He reports getting a couple of clients from people who never spent a dime on his services!

Step 3: Create a Calm, Clutter-Free Office Environment

Harry's premises are clutter-free, both physically but also audibly. People with gravitas do not have telephones ringing off the hook.

They're in charge of their environment and their time.

Step 4: Lighten the Mood With Something Fun

Yes, Harry wants to be seen as an authority, but it's easy to go too far and appear 'stuffy.' He wants respect. However, he also wants to convey a sense of fun. Who wants to work with someone who's boring?

Harry proudly displays his 'The Bean King' trophy, an old gift making fun of his coffee obsession.

> **Helpful Tip**
>
> Don't be afraid to show a little of your fun side by displaying a 'joke' award or a funny memento. The only people this will offend are dullards who you will hate working with anyway.
>
> For my 40th birthday, nine friends and I attended one of those pop video experience days. It was a memorable event. I decided to make it even more memorable by holding an 'awards ceremony' a month later.
>
> I found these cheap plastic Oscar-like awards on eBay. I gave them out on the night for best outfit, best dancer, sexiest twerker, etc.
>
> The sexiest twerker winner displays his award in his office. He's a respected environmental consultant.

Eliminating Sales Anxiety for Good

I started this chapter by recounting my experiences working for a window insulation firm where I learned selling is hard. Perhaps you also have an experience where you needed to sell and felt anxious, nervous and fearful? Most of us don't like selling and we hate being sold to.

I liken sales to someone badgering a person for a date when they're not flirting. Surely getting a date is far more comfortable when you read the signals first. And it's easier still if you can draw that person toward you, instead of chasing them.

I want to use the phrase 'attraction marketing' to explain how top entrepreneurs win dream clients or opportunities as this is what they do. But I dislike that term now as various online 'gurus' have hijacked it.

These gurus changed the term to mean attracting clients by being on social media 24/7. If constant marketing and lead generation is sapping your energy, you'll solve that problem in the next chapter, so stick around.

What I mean by attraction marketing is possessing the ability to draw dream clients and opportunities to you, instead of you chasing them. That's what people at the top of their game do. This is what my clients do. They do not need to sell. Their book eliminates the need to chase clients or opportunities, which means they experience no sales anxiety.

A salesperson repels people. An expert attracts people.

And the shorthand for an expert, in any market, language or country in the world, is a published author.

Chapter 3: Quiz

1. What is Diagnostic Selling?

    ☐ Eliminating selling by having the authority to diagnose instead.

    ☐ Immediately getting more sales calls.

    ☐ Never having to speak to potential clients on the phone again.

2. What can eliminate sales anxiety for good?

    ☐ Your authority-building book.

    ☐ An incredible salesperson that you hire.

    ☐ A great website that sells your services.

3. At which sales phase can you use the Zero Selling System?

    ☐ Just pre-sale.

    ☐ Pre-sale, peri-sale (during) and post-sale.

    ☐ Pre-sale and post-sale.

CHAPTER 4

LEVERAGE YOUR BOOK
TO GENERATE QUALIFIED LEADS

As a business owner, lead generation is the lifeblood of your business. I see far too many entrepreneurs concentrate on the quantity of leads they get, instead of the quality. This leads to depressingly low lead to client conversion rates. I know I'd choose 50 qualified leads over 1,000 cold leads any day.

The problem is that most business owners are ineffective at qualifying leads. This leads to them spending far too much time generating and chasing leads, without showing much return in time and investment. They're unable to keep their pipeline of prospects warm and progressing, which means they veer from feast to famine continually in their business.

However, when you know *how* to leverage your business book in the right way, you'll open the door to regular, reliable streams of qualified leads.

In this chapter:

- you'll learn why book content is far superior to all other forms of content for lead generation
- you'll discover how to leverage your book to create a bottomless well of evergreen content for social media
- you'll get a handy downloadable mind map of content generation ideas that are guaranteed to draw the best leads to you
- you'll discover a whole world of lead generation beyond social media

- you'll get a brilliant list of direct mail ideas designed for authors that generate qualified leads

- and you'll find out how to encourage some very influential people to generate leads *for* you

All Content is Not Equal

We live in an information overload era. There's now more information in the world than ever in the history of mankind.

This is why most online content doesn't command a lot of respect. It's the sheer amount of it.

Anyone can post on social media or write a blog post. That doesn't mean you should give up on social media. You just need to be clever.

What if you found a way to make it work for you? What would that look like? A smart way is to move your target audience away from the noise of the online world. A way to have them focused solely on you and your message. You can do this by leveraging your book.

Several years ago, I was in Berlin visiting The Empty Library at the Bebelplatz, one of many infamous Nazi book burning sites. The Empty Library consists of a glass plate set into the cobbles viewing vast empty bookcases large enough to hold 20,000 books. This is a memorial to the burnt books of 1933.

Can you imagine a memorial to televisions? Radios? Brochures and fliers? How about social media posts or sales pages? It would never happen.

No matter what culture you live in worldwide, all of them hold books with the kind of respect you never give to other forms of media. For example, you would never throw out unwanted books the way you throw out brochures or delete e-mails.

As The Empty Library proves, books can even be 'dangerous.' The information they hold can be powerful enough to transform people through education, something the Nazis were wary of and wished to suppress.

Compare this to the danger of television or social media. Here the perceived danger is the 'dumbing down' of people.

Books command respect. And when you're an author, *you* command respect too. Let's play an imaginary game of online knock-knock to see the difference:

> *Knock-knock!*
>
> *Who's there?*
>
> *A random person online giving you advice on a subject.*
>
> *Knock-knock!*
>
> *Who's there?*
>
> *The author of a controversial new book.*

Whose post would you stop and read?

Getting attention is only part of the solution. You want attention from qualified leads and not just anybody. When you leverage your book well, you will find it is the ultimate source of qualified leads for two reasons.

1) Your Book is Your Most Complete Marketing Message

I doubt anybody reads every single page of your website or blog. Or watches every video you make. Or consumes all your social media content.

But someone who reads your book consumes your message in its entirety. Who you are, what you stand for, why you do what you and more. (Even if they don't read your entire book, they're likely to bookmark where they stopped so they can come back to it at a later date. This never happens with your online content.)

A lead that comes from a book is far superior to all other leads because they understand you and what you can do for them intimately. By the time they raise their hand and ask for help, they're 'pre-sold' to working with you.

2) Your Marketing Message Has Been Honed to Perfection

By the time you publish your book, it is first written, then rewritten, then rewritten again. You'll hire editors, ask colleagues to review it, and seek out all manner of professional help.

Simply put, it's the most polished piece of marketing material you will create.

Compare that to a blog post or social media post. I doubt you spend much time reviewing and rewriting each post. Who has the time? And I doubt you have several eyes reviewing every single piece of content before you put it out there.

The content in your book is therefore far more powerful, thorough and persuasive.

In the next few pages, you'll discover leveraging strategies, both offline and online, that build a constant pipeline of warm prospects.

And, if you're sick of creating content without seeing any returns, let me show you how to hop off the content generation treadmill for good.

The Infinite Content Machine

Social media gurus tell you they have the key to magically attracting qualified leads. Instead of chasing leads, they'll be 'magnetized' toward you.

This is why most of us go down the content generation rabbit hole. Attraction marketing is all about sharing valuable content. Content that speaks directly to leads who are your ideal clients and gets them to seek you out.

Sounds awesome, doesn't it? I mean, who wants to chase leads?

You hear 'facts' about it taking seven 'touches' before someone will act upon your call to action. Therefore you exhaust yourself with content creation, social media posts, blogging, videos, etc.

Several months later, and no new clients were magically attracted to you. So now you're told the secret is content syndication. This is not just about posting something every single day. It's about being seen on as many different platforms as possible.

Off you go, blasting content to as many different platforms as possible. But it's not that simple. It never is. Different platforms have different rules regarding length, images, links, etc. So now you have to change content for each platform.

Is it any wonder that within a couple of months, you're worn out?

I have close contact with a lot of business owners. The vast majority report they only manage to post two to three times a week. They have a business to run. Who has the time to generate daily content and then syndicate it out?

Content generation is a job in itself. Even when you start to see some successes, the content generation grind never stops. You need to continue pumping out content for several months to see traction. And then you need to keep generating content to keep that traction.

Let's compare this to Josh's experience.

Case Study

Josh, an executive coach, opened his business 20 months before we co-wrote his book.

He used his book to target potential clients he met while networking. However, after exhausting this avenue, he still needed to generate more leads. With a fledgling business, he had zero time for content generation. So, we hatched a plan.

Josh hires a freelancer for roughly $700. They go through his entire book and edit it into posts for social media. This yields 500+ social media posts.

That's almost 18 months' worth, if he chooses to post every day. Ready to be drip-fed into Facebook and LinkedIn, as well as his website.

He could have stopped there. It would have been enough. But he wanted to go further. Again he hires a cheap freelancer, this time to go through these posts and pull out any quotes. The freelancer then turns them into inspirational image quotes for a couple of hundred dollars.

This yields 50+ of these images, which Josh schedules into his Instagram and Pinterest accounts.

Finally, he hires another freelancer to create videos from his posts. This one cost him around $1,000 as the freelancer needed to create professional videos. But, I'm sure you will agree, that's a small price to pay for a year and a half's worth of videos on YouTube that are continuously generating leads.

One book created around 18 months' worth of social media content for Josh, without any burnout.

But even that wasn't his trump card. Because guess what he did after he had used up his posts? He started all over again. Who would remember what he posted 18 months ago?

In other words, he never needs to generate content ever again. He now has what I call an Infinite Content Machine. He has all the posts, videos and images he could ever need. And he just recycles them.

He does create new content, now and again, when he feels good about it. Maybe he's inspired by a particular session with a client. Or he discovers a new development in his industry.

But he experiences no "I need to post something" anxiety or frustration. The content is all there at his fingertips.

This is how he built his business to a hugely successful coaching empire. And all with less than two years' experience under his belt.

Warning

In my experience, reusing social media content works very well. But reusing content that you used for e-mails can be problematic.

A couple of my clients have noticed that people pay more attention to their e-mails. This means a minority of people will have long memories and they may even complain that you are 'recycling' emails.

If you want to reuse e-mails or e-mail newsletters, rewrite them yourself or hire a freelancer to rewrite them for you.

Yes, this will cost you in either time or money, but it's worth it so you're not seen as someone who is rehashing content to send to your list.

If you choose to hire a freelancer, it should cost a fraction of normal charges for e-mail writing. Remember, you're not asking them to come up with new content, which takes time to research and create. All you're asking them to do is rewrite the content. Because of this, you should be able to secure a cheap rate.

Please keep in mind that cheap does not mean dirt cheap. Choose very cheap freelancers at your peril. Many of these freelancers will not speak English at a fluent level. This means you will need to read through their work and check for errors, which defeats the whole point of outsourcing this task.

Helpful Tip

Here are yet more ideas:

1. Create posts for Facebook, LinkedIn and your website or blog.

2. Turn posts into videos for YouTube.

3. Turn posts into podcasts.

4. Send posts to trade or specialist publications for publishing.

5. Send posts to leading bloggers for publishing.

6. Turn quotes into image quotes for Instagram and Pinterest.

7. Turn quotes into tweets for Twitter that link to website articles or blog posts.

8. Turn posts into e-mails or newsletters to send out to an e-mail list.

9. Turn posts into physical newsletters to mail out.

10. If content allows, turn posts into infographics to post on any social media.

11. If content allows, turn posts into slides to upload to places like SlideShare.

12. Use content in books as a foundation for radio shows, internet TV programs, etc.

The list above is not exhaustive. There are many other ways to disseminate the content out into the world.

The good news is, finding experts to help you do this and repurpose for different platforms is easy and cheap.

Hiring freelancers can be expensive when you're expecting them to be creative and create content from scratch. But when you have the content (i.e., your book), you'll find many technically gifted but reasonably priced technicians who can repurpose your content in creative ways.

If you write a book once, you'll have all the content you'll ever need to promote your business. Which would you choose? Write online content forever or write a book once?

> If you write a book once, you'll have all the content you'll ever need to promote your business.

Resource: Infinite Content Machine Mind Map

I created a handy, at-a-glance mind map showing you different ways you can repurpose content from your book. This is great to use yourself or delegate to someone else. Look for it in your free resources from:

- www.thefreedommasterplan.com/free-resources

The Sexiest Word in the English Language

As a copywriter, my job is to play with words and test the public's reaction. And the one word that pulls in leads like crazy, is the word 'free.'

Go to exhibitions and you'll see the 'free' phenomenon in action. Just spend half an hour studying people as they walk from one booth to the next.

In most cases, you'll see them take one freebie after another. I'll never know why anyone needs that many pens, key rings, and lanyards. But everyone does it. "It's free. Why not?"

And yet, brochures, leaflets, flyers, etc., are seen differently, despite being free. Free is only seductive when the item is valuable.

> *Free is only seductive when the item is valuable.*

Yes, you might accept marketing material. In most cases, you feel you have to oblige when they're being shoved in your face. Especially when they come with a free pen or something. However, if you stay until the end of an exhibition, you'll see an ocean of thrown-away marketing materials.

But not many pens.

A book falls into the same category as pens. Give it away for free, and it's almost guaranteed to be taken home because it's valuable. Plus, it does a far better job of selling you and your products and services than a pen or lanyard.

Now, I'm not suggesting you start giving out your book to anyone and everyone. You'll end up spending a fortune. *Who* gets your book is important.

Giving away free books can be a costly exercise if you don't target your audience. But what exhibitions demonstrate is the power of free when the free item is useful instead of 'marketing stuff.'

Let's look at a few tried and tested strategies my clients use to generate targeted leads, both online and offline.

Free Book Promotions for Lead Generation

Case Study

Josh is an executive coach with a fledgling 20-month-old business. He knows the leads he wants to target, not just a dream client avatar. He knows the exact people. Coming from a corporate world of many years, he kept an extensive network of executive-level acquaintances.

These would be ideal clients for his business.

Now, when I say acquaintances, I mean acquaintances. People he met at networking events. They may remember his face. But he was not buddies with them.

He couldn't just call them and say, "Hey, I set up my own executive coaching business, fancy being my client?" So he thought of a novel way to earn their attention.

He mails a copy of his book with a handwritten note saying, "I liked this book and thought you would too." He then signs off with only his first name.

He reports getting fantastic feedback. Executives are used to sifting through a lot of boring mail. A book with a handwritten note? To call that unusual is an understatement.

Many of his acquaintances get in touch to congratulate him on a great book. This opens the door to conversations about what he can offer them as an executive coach.

Helpful Tip

Many executives have 'gatekeepers' such as PAs and receptionists. These people go through their mail, sifting through to only leave what they think is essential. This means most executives never see most marketing material.

However, I'm sure you won't be surprised to know every single one of Josh's books end up in the hands of his acquaintances.

Remember, everyone views books as valuable, even non-readers.

Not one of these gatekeepers dare to throw away Josh's book. Instead, it gets put to the top of the 'must-read' pile.

If your dream clients, investors, donors, etc., are behind a wall of gatekeepers, be sure to utilize your business book to break through.

Josh knew the exact people he wanted to target, but not everyone is that lucky.

Here are some strategies when you don't know the exact people, but have a dream client avatar.

Trade Shows or Exhibitions

The key here is to find companies exhibiting in the show who are complementary to your business. Then, give those companies copies of your book to give out.

First of all, they save money as they need to give out fewer free gimmicks. Secondly, they're giving out something far more valuable than a free pen.

This makes them look great in front of potential clients.

At a trade show I attended a couple of years ago, I saw a booth where you had to leave your name and e-mail address for the free book. The book was not from this company. The book was from a 'strategic partner' i.e., someone savvy enough to contact this company to do their marketing for them. The list was for the company.

This company got to build a list of potential clients by giving away a book they didn't make. Something you could never do with basic freebies. Who would leave a name and e-mail for a pen? The strategic partner got his book given out to a targeted audience while not even attending.

If you do happen to be attending, why not do a book signing? People love these. The complementary business can promote an hour-long 'meet the author' slot at their booth. They earn a rush of people to their booth. You earn a rush of potential clients.

Events and Seminars

As with trade shows and exhibitions, you can find events in line with your book's topic. Contact the organizers and ask to add a free copy of your book to their goody bag.

Most events give out bags of freebies to attendees. Most organizers don't want to weigh their bags down with marketing material. A book, on the other hand, is much more likely to make them say yes.

I've seen organizers add in books from authors who were not even attending, such is the value of adding a free book. Books add weight to their goody bags, both figuratively and literally. And, if you are attending, you can use the power of a book signing hour.

> **Warning**
>
> Adding your book to event goody bags is a great strategy, but only if the event will attract your target audience. This is not a great strategy at large, general events.

Webinars or Teleseminars

It's easy to find webinars on Google. The organizers want to be found online by potential attendees.

I attended many webinars where there's an ethical bribe of some sort. "If you stay till the end, you'll get this complimentary report, course, software, etc." Organizers do this because all webinars and teleseminars lose a ton of attendees within the first 30 minutes.

The problem is many of these organizers don't have a bribe. Or they've got a poor one put together at the last minute. These creators would love a great bribe that motivates their attendees to stay till the end. A book from a published author is a real draw.

This is a great way to tap into someone else's audience and let them do the marketing for you.

> **Warning**
>
> Always research the audience of the webinar or teleseminar you're targeting. What you don't want is your book to be offered to thousands of people who are not your target audience.
>
> This can lead to you spending a ton of money on books without seeing a return on investment.

Associations, Memberships and Chambers of Commerce

Most industries and business niches have associations or memberships. Many are more than happy to feature a published author on their websites, social media profiles, etc.

The same follows for local chambers of commerce. Published authors are hugely respected. They'd love to shout about the fact that 'one of their own' is a published author.

You can also ask to send your book to members as a free perk. This may cost you several hundred books. Only do this when you know for sure that the members are your target audience. But if they *are* your target market, I can't imagine any association saying no to giving away a free, valuable book to their members. And without it costing them a dime.

Paid Adverts

Another route to targeted lead generation is to use adverts to promote your free book giveaway. Where you advertise depends on your target audience's comforts and your experience. You can choose online ads, such as Google ads or social media ads.

Additionally, you can choose to advertise in general print or specialist publications. There are also radio and TV adverts.

It's beyond this book's scope to go into the advantages and disadvantages of different forms of advertising. It's in your interest to research which advertising platforms reach your target audience the best.

Warning

When advertising a free book promotion, be sure to focus on your target audience. An advert that 'speaks' to everyone will be dangerous. Anyone could request a copy (like the free pens at an exhibition). Your ads need to spell out who your target is for your book.

A good screening process is to request a telephone number for someone to receive the book.

Use this with an advert that talks only to your target market. This will stop people who are not your target audience from requesting a copy. After all, you *might* follow up with a phone call.

Another screening process is to promote the book as free, but you charge for post and packaging. Again, this stops freebie seekers who are not in your target market.

It's worth testing to see which approach gets you the best returns.

Aditya, a life coach, uses free book promotions to great effect.

Case Study

In Aditya's locality, there are at least 200 other life coaches. She found it challenging to differentiate herself from the competition and find qualified leads.

So we wrote a book together that targeted her dream clients, which were high-flying female executives juggling a demanding career with young children.

She noticed that when she Googled for a life coach in her state, there were many ads from competitors. She decided to take a different approach and advertise her free book.

Imagine using Google to search for a coach in your area and finding a ton of ads promoting services. But then you see one ad offering a valuable book. Which would you click?

I'm sure you can see, this strategy was a great success for Aditya. When someone clicks on Aditya's ad, they go to her website to leave their name, address and phone number. Each time she runs the ad, she hires a temporary staff member for a couple of weeks to ring everyone who has requested a book.

This staff member takes each lead through a short questionnaire that verifies they are in Aditya's target market. From this, she secures on average two new high paying dream clients worth thousands of dollars each per annum.

But that's not where the story ends.

Aditya's ad comes to the president's attention of the local chapter of a national female entrepreneurs networking group. Impressed with the book, this lady contacts Aditya to ask if she would speak at their next monthly meeting.

Aditya does a little research on this networking group. She finds that it's full of high-level female CEOs and executives. In other words, her dream clients.

She finds out how many would attend and makes sure she has enough books for every attendee. The one speech Aditya gives to a small group of 20 attendees allows her to pick up one long-term client.

But the buzz she creates by giving away her book to all attendees gets the national president's attention. She now spends one weekend a month traveling to different states speaking to local chapters of this national group. Each time she speaks, she picks up new dream clients.

Before we co-wrote her book, Aditya ran ads where she gave away various free items to attract leads. She's tried free reports and even free 30-minute consultations.

To date, she states nothing has performed as well as her book.

Newsletters

Earlier in this chapter, you discovered how you could disseminate your book into a ton of content, including newsletters. However, you can also tap into the newsletter audience of a complementary business.

Many companies publish weekly or monthly newsletters, either by e-mail or direct mail (or both). They're continually looking for interesting information to add to their newsletters.

Most of them don't know what you know. They don't know that books will give you all the content you could ever need. They don't have a book. This means they're on that content generation treadmill.

Getting done-for-you content is a godsend for them. You have all this content. Why not leverage it further and give them access to it so you can access their leads and clients?

You can make it even more appealing by offering to feature *their* content in *your* newsletter if you have one. This strategy works well for any content that grabs interest in your target audience. But it works well in combination with a free book promotion.

Drive people from these newsletters to your website, landing page or wherever they can order a copy of your book for free. If people have read a little of your content in a newsletter, they're likely to be interested in additional content from the book.

Of course, you need to do your due diligence and check their audience is also your target audience. Also, there's nothing to stop you from being interviewed, should you wish or are asked. Everyone loves interviewing a respected author.

Social Media

Finally, the last way to use free book promotions is via social media.

There's a lot of emphasis on creating connections on social media, which is great. The problem is you could waste a ton of time chatting to people without any return on time invested. The idea is to turn those conversations into leads or opportunities.

The best way to do this is to move these potential leads to somewhere you can collect their information. A great example is a landing page that collects information from them in exchange for something valuable.

Yet again, offering a book works like gangbusters, compared to the typical PDFs, reports, etc. Just remember to screen the requests. You don't want to spend money on timewasters.

The great thing here is that social media is quite transparent. All you have to do is click on someone's profile to see if they are in your target audience.

Case Study

Sean, a marketing consultant, created free online training as a lead generation tool. He decides to split test this with the book I co-wrote with him.

Half of his social media posts promote the free online training offer, while the other half promote the book. He offers the book for free, like his online training. However, he asks for $4.99 to cover post and packaging.

Despite this extra cost, the book out-performs his free online training by two to one.

But that's not the end of the story.

The real 'magic' happens several weeks later. The leads that ask for the free book are four times more likely to buy his high ticket consultancy offer than those who take up the free training.

Never Overlook Direct Mail for Lead Generation

Did you know, of the 500 richest people on the Forbes 500 list, less than 50 don't use direct mail? The remaining 450+ are all using this so-called outdated form of lead generation.

So the next time you hear that direct marketing is dead, ask that person if they're in the Forbes 500. Hopefully, that should shut them up. I can spend the next hour throwing statistic after statistic at you. However, I'll prove my point faster by getting you to think about your habits.

Right now, how many unopened e-mails do you think you have in your inbox? Ten? 100? More? Now, how many envelopes or parcels are waiting for you on your doormat or mailbox? Not many, right?

I bet you're like most people and go through your mail every day. Or at the very least a couple of times a week. Even the mail you don't open, you don't leave it lying on your doormat or in your mailbox, correct? You see it, you register it as 'junk,' and you throw it in the bin.

Now think of how many e-mails you have waiting for you that you never even sent to the bin. Never mind those that might be interesting enough to open.

While idiots say "direct mail is dead," smart entrepreneurs use it to generate qualified leads that convert into clients. Because the online world has become so crowded, you have to shout louder and louder to win any attention. Meanwhile, it's quiet enough to hear a pin drop in peoples' mailboxes.

Once you get started, instead of getting annoyed at these direct mail cynics, you'll secretly want to kiss them. Because the more they convince others that direct mail is dead, the bigger the opportunity you have offline.

Why Your Book is a Direct Marketing Dream

I want you to think about the mail you think is 'junk' and throw away without opening. Why do you think it's junk? Perhaps you recognized the branding on the envelope and knew who it was?

There's one catalog firm that I bought a dress from about five years ago. Despite not buying anything from them since, they send me marketing material about once a month. As soon as I see it, I know what it is, and off it goes to the bin.

Perhaps other details give the game away?

For me, if I see anything that says "To the occupier," I immediately think junk. I bet you too have a junk radar. You probably have a mental list of telltale signs built up over the years to help you sift mail fast.

But one thing that completely bypasses the radar, no matter how 'junk-like' the envelope or parcel, is lumpy mail. As soon as you feel something lumpy inside the envelope, you have to open it to investigate.

You may throw out everything inside. But I'm yet to meet anyone that throws away a lumpy envelope without opening it. This is why big corporations add things like pens, key rings, fobs or other cheap promotional material inside their envelopes.

They know it guarantees people will open their envelopes.

But that does not mean everyone reads the marketing materials inside. I open lumpy mail out of curiosity, as do most people. I then decide whether the item is worth keeping or not.

A pen is always handy, so I'll keep it. That doesn't mean I will read the contents of the envelope. Yes, there's a higher chance of me doing so as I've opened the envelope. But there's no guarantee I will read it.

Having a pen around my house with particular branding is good for the company. Because at some point, if I do need their products or services, they're likely to be top of mind.

I assume that's why these companies spend extra money to add their branding instead of sending out unbranded items. But as a business owner, you want a more immediate return on your investment.

This is why I would never advise you to send out gimmicky promotional stuff in the mail. This approach might work for large corporations with deep pockets. But it's not for us.

Remember, promotional items are just that, for promoting something. Or in other words, selling. Earlier you discovered why people snap up things like free pens at trade shows and exhibitions. But that doesn't necessarily mean they will become customers of the brand.

They know that this free promotional stuff is ultimately a sales tactic. And they act accordingly (i.e., they take the freebie and run).

Now compare that to a book.

Imagine getting a lumpy envelope in the mail and you feel the heft of a book. Of course, you're going to open it. You then find a professional-looking book with a letter. Are you going to read the letter and flick through the book? Of course you are!

First of all, you won't throw it away. Because who throws away a book? Even if you don't wish to keep a book, you give it away to others, sell it or donate it. But no one throws books away. Books have an innate worth that makes that unthinkable.

Secondly, this isn't some promotional item that you know is trying to get you to buy something. It's a book. A source of knowledge and wisdom. A gift.

I'm not suggesting you start sending out books *en masse* unless you have deep pockets or want to go bankrupt. But sending books in the mail works wonders for generating leads from targeted audiences.

Case Study

Harry, a financial consultant, speaks at different seminars and events because of the book we co-wrote.

Some of these seminars are huge and attract 1000+ attendees. These attendees come from a wide variety of career backgrounds. But other seminars are smaller and more targeted.

One event in particular was a small exclusive event held for CEOs of mid-size companies. This was Harry's target audience.

After impressing them with his first speech, he's asked to speak regularly at their events. He even becomes a paid-up member of their organization.

Part of the membership benefits is having access to a list of members with their contact details for networking. He could have done what many do. He could just give out his book to people at each event he spoke to for this organization.

But Harry is hungry for immediate success. He decides to send out his book via direct mail to every member.

The envelope is plain, but the 'lumpiness' from his book meant everyone opens it. To make sure no one would accidentally throw it out, Harry adds a 'Free Book Inside' graphic on the envelope.

Who in their right mind would throw that away?

The response is fantastic. Nearly every envelope is opened. Harry gets so many leads that he has to take on a new staff member to handle it all. And all because he uses direct mail for lead generation.

Warning

Sending your book out to a mailing list only works when the list is targeted to your dream client, investor, collaborator, etc.

Harry speaks at many events, but he chose this approach for this particular organization only.

Why? Because over time, he found out this organization had many of his dream clients. At events where he has a more mixed crowd, he does not utilize this approach.

Sending out books in the mail can be a costly exercise. Harry makes sure his books only go out to people he knows are his target audience.

Helpful Tip

Another approach is to ask your publisher or editor to send the book on your behalf.

This isn't something any of my former clients have done. But I've been told that it works very well and I can imagine why.

It adds to the gravitas of an author. They're so busy with their important work. They couldn't possibly have time to send out books. So instead, they have their trusted publisher or editor sidekick to do it for them.

Don't worry. If you can't target precisely, that doesn't mean you can't tap into the power of direct marketing.

Read on to see how Liz overcame this issue.

Case Study

Liz, a fitness coach, does not have a targeted list of people for leads. She decides to search for mailing lists full of her target audience (middle-aged women fighting middle-aged spread). This is easily done by going somewhere like SRDS.com. Here you can generate lists with targeting options, such as gender, age, location, etc.

She sends a letter enclosed in an envelope marked "From the author of the groundbreaking book." The envelope also mentions the title of the book. The title spells out how this book helps middle-aged women lose their bulge without starvation.

Her direct mail wasn't even lumpy, but it still got a great response.

She was sensible and started small by mailing to 500 women. The cost was around $500 ($1 per envelope). Out of this, she got 200+ responses, with 23 turning into $25 per month clients.

Within the first month, the new clients paid for her direct mail experiment. By month two, it was pure profit.

Resource: Direct Mail Ideas

Direct mail works – period. But what dramatically increases conversions are ideas that tie in with your elevated status as an author.

Check the Resources section near the back of the book for the link.

Books are the ultimate dream when it comes to direct marketing.

First, there is barely any competition for attention compared to the online world. When someone is online, it's like they're being shouted at by hundreds of salespeople at every turn. Offline is far quieter. And second, you're able to trump any competition you *do* have within direct mail, because of the authority you gain as a published author.

Imagine you receive three envelopes in the post.

One has branding, which immediately screams, "I want to sell you something."

The second has something small and lumpy inside. This one screams, "I want to sell you something, please open because I have a freebie to give you."

The third is lumpy because it has a book. It quietly says, "I'm representing an expert and authority who feels this information will be beneficial to you."

If these three envelopes were people, who would you let into your home?

Generating Leads From Free Publicity

Earlier you discovered how most media, such as brochures, sales pages, etc., are seen as marketing materials. Their sole purpose is to sell. You found that the perception of books is different. They are a source of valuable expert information. Therefore, books cleverly bypass the cynical brain designed to shut out marketing messages.

The good news is, books have a similar effect on TV producers, radio producers, newspaper and magazine editors, bloggers and a whole host of other influential people.

This allows you to tap into the kind of free publicity that money (literally) cannot buy. You can encourage these powerful, influential people to generate leads for you.

Let me explain.

Say you'd love your local newspaper to feature you. How do you do that? One option is to pay for an ad. This can certainly fetch some attention.

But you know that the average person tunes out marketing messages. A more intelligent way might be to advertise a book instead of your business or products and services. But what if you didn't need to pay for an ad at all?

What if you could have your local newspaper do an editorial piece about your business?

This kind of publicity beats every type of paid advertising you can think of for lead generation. It will even beat an advert for a *free* book promotion. Because adverts scream 'selling.' But an editorial is educational, like a book.

This is why many companies create adverts that *look like* editorial pieces in newspapers and magazines. These are called 'advertorials.' Advertorials became very problematic several years ago in the UK.

Many people complained when they found out an article was an advert. Because of this, The Advertising Standards Agency forced newspapers and magazines to put a headline above advertorials. Advertisers had to state that their 'editorial' was a paid promotion (in other words, an advert).

I see similar disclaimers on American cable channels when late-night infomercials take over. And yet, despite the public being aware of these paid promotions, these editorial-adverts *still* convert far higher than outright adverts.

However, if you can win a *genuine* editorial, this is by far the best publicity you will ever get. And you can achieve that with a book.

Allow me to demonstrate with a friend of mine, Justin, who is a career coach.

Case Study

Justin has been in business for around five years with some good clients, and he's ready to be in the news. But how is this an exciting news piece?

Even if he just opened his business, what's so great about this? Where is the news angle? Opening your business, reaching a milestone, expansion plans, etc., might be fantastic news for you. But to an editor, that isn't anything to make them sit up and take notice.

Sadly for you, all they care about is giving their readers interesting and informative content. You need to bring some sort of interest.

So perhaps you're doing lots of free work in the community? Maybe you're fundraising for a local charity? Things like that are newsworthy. But that sort of thing takes a lot of time and energy which Justin did not have.

Instead, he informs his local newspaper he is publishing a book. A book about the three reasons why people make wrong career moves that lead to depression.

Think about it. Which article would you want to read? "Local career coach celebrates five years in business." Or "Local career coach: three ways your job choices are making you sick."

Your book doesn't have to be as dramatic as Justin's book. You are someone credible and worth listening to just by being a published author. It doesn't only work on newspaper and magazine editors. It also works for a whole host of influential people. Your book *is* your news angle. Use it.

> *Your book is your news angle. Use it.*

Media Machine

Follow these steps to create what I call a Media Machine that will generate publicity and leads for years to come.

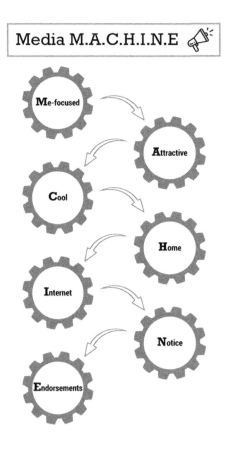

Figure 4: Media M.A.C.H.I.N.E

Step 1: Become Me-Focused

It might seem like there are too many media outlets out there. Cut down on overwhelm by becoming 'me-focused.'

What radio shows do you listen to often? What local TV channels do you tune in to watch? Which bloggers do you follow? Start with who interests you.

You'll find that, because you genuinely like these media outlets, this comes across when you contact them. Once you're featured there, you'll be amazed at how opportunity comes knocking on your door from other outlets.

Step 2: Become Attractive to the Media

You know the drill by now. The book is not the business. You're leveraging your book to boost your authority. This allows you to charge higher fees, as well as open up other revenue streams.

So don't be stingy. Make yourself attractive by giving your book away for free to producers, journalists, bloggers, reviewers and key influencers.

Step 3: Keep Your Cool

Just like the steady tortoise wins the race over the hare, think of your Media Machine as something that builds up over time.

One client burned out because she said yes to every local TV show, radio show and interview offer she got. This would make sense if her book was topical. But she's a life coach. People will continue to need life coaches for a long time to come.

Yes, traditional media tend to view a new book as 'newsworthy' for the first three months after release. But there's nothing to stop you creating a second edition later on. This allows you to win media attention again.

So take it steady and let the momentum build up.

Step 4: Start Close to Home

Yes, you might dream of being featured on Fox News. Or having your smiling face in The New York Times. But it's much easier to start with low hanging fruit.

I'm not saying you shouldn't aim for the stars. But starting small will eventually attract the attention of the nationals if you keep at it. Plus, it's far less scary to practice with local players than go straight to the nationals (yikes)!

Resource: Vegans in the Limelight

I've been able to generate quite a lot of media buzz with my book, all due to the fantastic Vegans in the Limelight program.

Becoming an author is itself far more newsworthy than most other business owners. But that 'newsworthiness' doesn't stick for long.

Through this program by the incredible Katrina Fox from Vegan Business Media, I've learned about 'newsjacking' and how to use it for ongoing, regular coverage for months, if not years, after the launch of a book.

Check out Vegans in the Limelight here:

- www.thefreedommasterplan.com/limelight

Step 5: Don't Ignore the Internet

You'll be amazed how much reach you can gain being interviewed on a well-known local website. Or a blog. Or by a social media influencer. YouTube has incredible reach. Younger audiences spend more time watching YouTube than traditional TV channels. There are huge YouTube channels that rival and beat the viewer numbers of big TV networks.

As I said previously, start small and work your way up. So if there is a local YouTube channel in your target market, offer your book to review.

You can even allow them to give your book out. These content creators live and die by the number of viewers they get. They love doing giveaways, especially a book for its high perceived value, to increase viewer numbers and keep people watching them.

Step 6: Give Notice to Media Outlets

If you are speaking at a seminar, conference or other event, make sure you give local media outlets plenty of notice.

Local media love covering events.

First, find out if the organizer has contacted the media for coverage. If they haven't, ask permission to do so. You'll find many are more than happy that you're so proactive in getting the word out about their event.

Ideally, send a press release to these media outlets. This drastically increases the chances of them attending and featuring the event in their content.

Step 7: Ask for Endorsements

Again, this is much easier when you're operating on a local scale. It's very likely you know other business owners in your area. Perhaps you cross-referred clients or maybe you have relationships with other businesses. This is the time to give these people free copies.

People love to give endorsements because it allows them to bask in the reflected glory. Now, not only do they know a great published author, they have a mention on the front or back cover!

Automated Lead Generation From a Book

You can leverage your book to generate the hottest leads for your business.

So far, you discovered how a book can create an Infinite Content Machine that attracts clients to you. Your book contains all the social media and website content you could ever need to *permanently* generate publicity, dream clients, strategic partners, investors, etc., for your business.

Instead of running on the content treadmill forever, you do the work once. And then you leverage the work for years to come.

Your book also gives you the authority, celebrity and expert status that gets your content noticed in a sea of noise online. In a crowded market, promoting a book as a tool for lead generation makes you stand out.

Flip through any trade journal or magazine in your target market, you'll see advert after advert promoting similar products and services to yours. However, by running an ad promoting your book, you appear completely different from your competitors.

The public views you as an authority and expert because you're offering a valuable book. In the meantime, you attract highly qualified leads.

And finally, you found out that influential people in the media are also impressed by authors. Using the Media Machine steps, you can encourage these people to generate leads for you.

The good news is, once you start cranking up these 'machines,' they generate leads on autopilot for you. Once you start contacting media outlets for free publicity, this exposure gets other media outlets' attention. Which then brings the attention of more. The same goes for any of the ideas in this chapter. Exposure gets you more exposure.

I have clients who can't stop their machines, even if they tried. Many months later, they're still getting requests for interviews. Or to speak, to contribute to a webinar and so forth. They find themselves in the enviable position of having to turn down lead generating opportunities.

Is there such a thing as genuinely automated lead generation? Not if you want it immediately.

But if you put in a little effort to begin adopting one of the strategies, it will gain you and your business exposure and publicity. And it's this exposure and publicity that will allow you to generate leads on autopilot.

In the upcoming summary chapter, you're going to discover how to push this exposure and publicity into overdrive for rapid recognition and respect.

Chapter 4: Quiz

1. What is the sexiest word in the English Language?
   - ☐ Free.
   - ☐ You.
   - ☐ Buy.

2. What is an Infinite Content Machine?
   - ☐ An outsourced company that creates all your content for you.
   - ☐ Leveraging a book to create content once and then never needing to create again.
   - ☐ Needing to create content infinitely for social media.

3. Which of these is *not* one of the steps inside the Media Machine?
   - ☐ Ask for endorsements.
   - ☐ Start local.
   - ☐ Only focus on traditional media.

CHAPTER 5

SUMMARY: LEVERAGING YOUR BOOK FOR THOUGHT LEADERSHIP

I want to congratulate you for getting here. You've gone through nearly 80% of my book. You digested every single strategy on how to leverage a business book. You discovered how to use it to attract your dream clients.

You learned how it allows you to increase fees while also building passive income streams. And you found out how to leverage your book to remove sales anxiety, as well as turn it into an incredible lead generation tool.

Implementing any of the strategies outlined will build you the kind of authority that places you head and shoulders above your competition.

But perhaps you want more for yourself?

Although the phrase 'thought leader' has been around for over a century, it's become a buzzword only in the last couple of decades. As a published author, if you leverage your book well, the world will see you as an authority and trusted expert. A thought leader is the next level above this.

When you think of thought leaders, such as Tony Robbins in the US or Brad Burton in the UK, it's not just that they are experts in their field. They are the experts' expert. An authority above authorities. The person other experts look up to.

If the idea of becoming a thought leader seems farfetched, the truth is, if you're an author, you're closer than you think.

Would-be thought leaders need a great product, service, company or program. And they need a community of people, such as clients, customers, collaborators, strategic partners, etc. In the previous chapters, you discovered a host of tips and strategies to leverage your business book that attracts these influential people into your life. In other words, you're ahead.

What thought leadership status will do is act as a catalyst that brings more of these people into your life, and even automates the process.

Thought leadership is your next logical step.

In this chapter:

- you'll discover the benefits of becoming a thought leader
- you'll find the easiest way to become a sought-after thought leader and authority in your field
- and you'll get your downloadable Authority Catalyst Speech Template for the fastest results

The Benefits of Becoming a Thought Leader

Increase Publicity at an Exponential Rate

Previously, you learnt how you can leverage your book to attract the attention of media outlets. But once you achieve thought leadership status, the tables turn.

Media outlets start to chase you. More reporters, bloggers and influential people will reach out to you because you are a thought leader.

Do you think Toby Robbins contacts the media to cover his latest book or his upcoming event? Or do you think the media reaches out to him?

Being a thought leader fuels your PR opportunities, to the point that opportunities seek you out, rather than the other way around.

Create Rapid Trust and Credibility

You're aware that being a published author goes a long way with others seeing you as trustworthy and credible. As a thought leader, this is magnified. You'll find people refer you to others even when they're not a client or collaborator.

A few years ago, a colleague of mine recommended I attend a Robert Kiyosaki event. When I asked my colleague what Kiyosaki's events were like, he replied, "I don't know. I've never been. But I heard he's fantastic."

Boost Online Visibility

Online visibility is key for anyone marketing their business in the modern world. Which means many people have to create content on a prolific level. It's easy to run out of ideas. One way for these people to create content is by featuring thought leaders.

Do a Google search for a thought leader you like. You may find a couple of websites owned by the thought leader, perhaps some links to their social media, etc. But you'll also find articles and blog posts from various content creators featuring the thought leader.

I discussed earlier how you can use your book to encourage influential people, such as bloggers, to promote you. But as a thought leader, you'll find people feature you without you needing to ask them.

Aditya, a life coach who has become a thought leader, tells me she can't keep up with the number of articles and blog posts that are created about her. She doesn't know most of these content creators, and yet they are helping her build her online visibility and authority status.

How to Be a Thought Leader

To be a thought leader, you need to consistently share your knowledge and expertise with the world. This can be done in a number of ways, such as having a great online presence. But nothing marks you out as a candidate for thought leadership as much as public speaking.

When you think of the thought leaders that I mentioned, such as Robbins, Burton or Kiyosaki, I bet you picture them on a stage, correct? Inspiring and motivating a crowd that hangs on their every word.

No matter how many articles they write, podcasts they do, videos they create, etc., nothing has the same impact as public speaking. As Ralph Waldo Emerson said, "Speech is power."

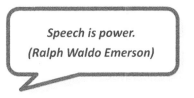

Speech is power.
(Ralph Waldo Emerson)

You may have heard that public speaking is the number one fear, pushing *death* down to the second position.

According to stand-up comedian and actor, Jerry Seinfeld, "This means to the average person, if you go to a funeral, you're better off in the casket than doing the eulogy!"

Jokes aside, it does demonstrate how frightening public speaking can be. However, if you want to accelerate your authority level to thought leadership status, speaking is the fastest route.

This is why I call speaking the Authority Catalyst. Follow the steps below and you'll be speaking like a pro in no time.

3S Stage Success

Figure 5: 3S Stage Success

Start Small

Most people are not likely to win a huge national stage straight off the bat.

Even if you are relatively well-connected and could pull strings to speak on a big stage, I recommend you start local. It allows you to 'get your feet wet,' make mistakes and be more comfortable with speaking.

All those assured orators at various seminars and events? Chances are they were very nervous when they started out. They just learned their craft to such an extent they can hide their nerves well. As Mark Twain once said, "There are only two types of speakers in the world. The nervous and liars."

> *There are only two types of speakers in the world. The nervous and liars.*
>
> *(Mark Twain)*

So give yourself a break. Start small and allow yourself to trip up. Each time you speak, you're only going to get better.

Join Your Local Speech Club

Networking clubs that allow members to give speeches, such Toastmasters clubs or 4Networking in the UK, provide an excellent place to start speaking. The great thing is, you can talk about any subject.

For your first time, you might find self-promotion too much. Certainly, having a published book helps, as the focus shifts from promoting you to promoting the book.

But if you're extra nervous, you don't need to talk about you or your business at all. You can talk about any subject you want, such as current affairs, a hobby, etc.

Speak Online

There's a whole world of speaking opportunities that do not involve being on an actual stage. There are:

- webinars or teleseminars

- internet TV channels
- internet radio channels
- podcasts
- local radio shows
- local TV shows

These allow you to hone your speaking skills without the scary image of hundreds of eyes trained on you.

Helpful Tip

If you're very nervous, start with pure audio platforms, such as telesemi-nars, podcasts, radio and audio-only social networking platforms.

Not being seen can give you confidence (no one will see you mopping your brow). You can progress on to more visual platforms as your confi-dence grows.

How easy is it to land a spot on these platforms? You'll be surprised, espe-cially as a published author.

These platforms are run by people who need to keep spewing out content at a prolific rate. They gladly welcome anybody who can help them. A published author is a big coup because of the news angle.

Content creators are always asking themselves, "Where's the news angle?" They want to provide their listeners or viewers with exciting and informative content.

You may want to talk about how great your business is. Unfortunately, that's not news for them. But when you approach them with a book which you want to discuss, *that* is news.

Finding these platforms is a piece of cake. The owners of these platforms make it easy for anyone to find them so they can increase the number of listeners or viewers. Simply Google your target market and then add the qualifier 'podcast' or 'radio channel' to the end.

> **Resource: Authority Catalyst Speech Template**
>
> It's easy to believe that a great speaker is born with an innate ability to speak. You may be surprised to know that many well-known speakers suffered major anxiety before becoming celebrated speakers.
>
> The secret for their success? A proven speech outline. A well-structured speech outline will give you the confidence to make memorable speeches that dramatically boost your authority, marking you as a thought leader. The link is in the Resources section near the back of the book.

Get Gigs

One of the biggest mistakes would-be speakers make is solely focusing on their own needs. What they should be doing is focusing on the needs of the event planner or promoter.

You're ahead of the curve.

Going through this book, you learned to put yourself in the shoes of newspaper editors, podcast hosts, etc. You learned that promoting your business might be a number one priority for you. But it holds no weight for them.

And you also learned that publishing a book gives them what they need. It gives them something newsworthy, interesting and educational. While, at the same time, it promotes you and your business.

Therefore, to be hired for the best speaking engagements, you also need to look at the promoter's needs. You need to satisfy those needs before your own.

Your book itself will go a long way in meeting these needs. But there are a few 'ninja' tactics that will allow you to win the best speaking gigs around.

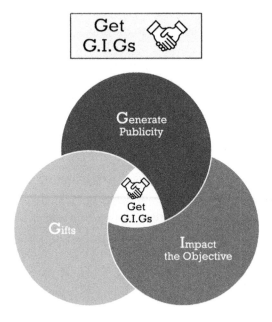

Figure 6: Get G.I.Gs

Prove You Can Generate Publicity for the Promoter

The number one priority for a promoter is bottoms on seats. They need to ensure they fill the venue and earn a great return on investment with tickets sold.

Too many speakers think their job is to stand there and give a speech. This can be true if you made a name for yourself as a speaker. Or if you are a celebrity in another field, such as sports, films, etc.

But when you're starting out, assuming you can win speaking engagements with a snap of a finger is naive.

You have the edge because you're a published author. That in itself puts you head and shoulders above other speakers who are not authors. But one way to ensure you beat other published authors is to demonstrate you understand a promoter's need to fill seats. And more importantly, you're willing to help them with this task.

If you have a mailing list, let them know that you will mail to promote their event. If you're active on social media, offer to promote their event on your profiles.

If you have any upcoming interviews on radio, podcasts, magazines, etc., explain you will mention their event at every opportunity.

Helpful Tip

Event organizers have a difficult job. Make their life as easy as possible by giving them everything they need to market you.

Give them your author biography, book synopsis, book reviews, testimonials or whatever you have that promotes you, your book and your business.

They need to sell you to their audience as a 'must-see' which means spending time creating event marketing and promotional content. Someone thoughtful enough to make this chore easier for them is a hero in their eyes.

Need help creating this?

The Ultimate Press Pack Toolkit for New Authors has everything you could possibly need to promote your book, grab media attention and boost sales and publicity, including templates for author biographies, book synopsis, speaker sheet, book cheat sheet, etc.

There are 18 pre-formatted, industry-standard templates, with worked examples, for even the most demanding international media organizations.

You'll also receive the What to Do When You Can't Afford a Publicist book. Inside, you'll receive step-by-step instructions on how to use the templates and exactly how to use your press pack to get as much media attention as you can handle, even if you have zero public relations experience.

Check the Resources section at the end of the book for the link or visit:

- www.thefreedommasterplan.com/press-pack-toolkit

Make an Impact on the Promoter's Objectives

Many speakers overlook this, which means you can use this insider information to your advantage. Find out exactly what the promoter wants to convey with their event. Then, slant your speech so it aligns with their message.

I'm not saying you have to change who you are completely. Never do that. Most of us instinctively distrust people who 'change with the wind.' Of course, your core values and thoughts should stay the same.

But you will find different events have different objectives. Let the promoter know that you know their objectives, and you're willing to help fulfil them and make an impact. Now you're no longer just a speaker. You're a valuable ally.

Bring Extra Value via Gifts

People love getting gifts at events. This is why many events give away goody bags on the first day at registration. Yet again, being a published author helps. You're not adding yet more marketing materials to their bags. You're adding a valuable book.

Let them know you're happy to give the book away for free to attendees (if the attendees are your target market). Or sell your book at an exclusive, 'just for this event' discount.

Helpful Tip

You know the power of a book signing by now. You could tell the event organizer that you can bring extra 'buzz' to their event by doing a book signing.

People love meeting authors and getting books signed!

Modesty is Not a Virtue

Society tells us modesty is a virtue and self-promotion a vice. Hollywood heroes never brag about how amazing they are. Instead, they're fawned over by the supporting cast. The villain is arrogant, and that is what brings about their downfall.

If you win an award, I bet you become self-effacing, thanking everybody on the planet despite knowing the primary reason for your success is your own blood, sweat and tears.

Self-promotion can be tough. Which is why you need to leverage your book. When you do this, a subtle and yet massive psychological shift happens. You're no longer promoting yourself, which can be panic-inducing. You're promoting a book.

You're no longer on a public stage trying to convince people you're great. You're an esteemed author who's merely expanding on the points in your book.

Thought leadership is not thrust on someone. The great thought leaders of the world made a choice to become one. They chose to promote themselves and elevate themselves to thought leadership status.

No one is going to ask you to be a thought leader. This is a choice that you make. Will you choose to become a thought leader?

The next chapter is a bonus for those without a book.

I wrote The Freedom Master Plan for existing authors as well as those who needed the motivation to write a book. If you're a published author, you can skip the bonus chapter.

Instead, pick the strategies that resonated with you inside The Freedom Master Plan and start implementing them. Your book is the best marketing and advertising tool you have at your disposal.

But *only* if you leverage it. So stop procrastinating and do it.

I'd love to hear your success stories.

Email me at:

- mitali@thefreedommasterplan.com

For the rest of you, the upcoming bonus chapter will show you how to write an authority-building, client-attracting, sales-anxiety-eliminating book.

Chapter 5: Quiz

1. Define Authority Catalyst:
   - ☐ Giving away books at record speed to win respect and recognition.
   - ☐ Using public speaking as a way to win accelerated respect and recognition.
   - ☐ Getting bestseller status to win respect and recognition.

2. Which of these is *not* a Get Gigs step?
   - ☐ Prove you can generate publicity for the promoter.
   - ☐ Refuse to bring extra value via gifts.
   - ☐ Make an impact on the promoter's objectives.

3. Which of these is *not* a virtue?
   - ☐ Modesty.
   - ☐ Patience.
   - ☐ Integrity.

HOW TO WRITE AN AUTHORITY-BUILDING BOOK

A full step-by-step instruction manual on how to write a business book is beyond the scope of this book.

I wrote The Freedom Master Plan to demonstrate how anyone can leverage a book to establish themselves as an authority and eliminate core problems they may face, such as lead generation, sales anxiety, etc. I wanted to show how vegan and ethical experts, influencers and entrepreneurs can use a book to gain visibility and exposure so they can put their mission, movement and message on the map.

However, I'm aware that there will be many people reading this book who are not published authors. Yet.

Perhaps this book has motivated you to finally put pen to paper. If that's you, here are the basic steps I go through when planning and writing a book.

Let's begin!

Define Your Knowledge and Experience

In this step, I want you to consider your knowledge and experience. You probably have a handful of ideas you could turn into books and I want you to think about which one will interest you most.

During the research phase, if you can feel yourself tiring of your topic, that should set off alarm bells. If you can feel your excitement building during the research, then that's a great sign you made the right choice.

Add Your Personality

Make the most of your personality in your book. Use:

- your life story and experiences
- your tone of voice
- your way of describing something

This is a great way to make your book different.

In real life, you use body language and intonation for emphasis. You can speak slowly or quickly. You can speak loudly or quietly. You can demonstrate a process with hand gestures. You can lean forward and whisper to share a secret.

With your book, you only have pages, pictures and paragraphs to convey your information. That's why bringing your personality into your writing is so important.

Don't put yourself on a pedestal and end up with a dry, authoritarian tone. You can avoid this by:

- writing using the same words and turns of phrase that you use when speaking face-to-face with someone
- adding feature boxes with attention-grabbing anecdotes
- injecting a little humor with some light-hearted snippets or cartoons about your trials and tribulations as you mastered your subject

This adds warmth to your book. People have an opportunity to discover more about the real you. As they read, they grow to know, like and trust you as the author, because you are upfront and honest about yourself, your experiences and your subject expertise.

Define Readers' Needs

Remember, your book isn't all about you. This is also about your readers. Readers' needs are simply the things that your readers want to know and the goals they hold.

You can define them by using the following phrase

1. as a… type of person,
2. I need… to know or be able to,
3. so I can… have a useful result.

Here is an example for a life coach for executive level working moms:

1. as a… executive in the corporate world,
2. I need to… learn how to balance my work and home life,
3. so I can… free myself from the guilt of not spending enough time with my child, while also giving them the best financial start in life.

Think about who your readers are, what they want to know and why it matters to them. That way you can make sure you write a book that has value for your readers, stays on track and gets you the credibility boost you deserve.

Research Bestselling Books

Have a look at other bestselling books on your subject. How did they describe and lay out their information to meet readers' needs?

Things to keep in mind:

- How did they organize the information? What is the sequence followed? What level of depth did they go to?
- Did they use pictures to explain particular points or did they rely on words?
- Did they provide any quizzes, templates, forms or exercises to help the reader feel confident they are mastering the topic and making good progress?

Education Above All Else

Now you know the secret. An authority-building book is really a sales mechanism. However, it's so ingenious that it flies under the 'sales radar' for everyone.

But that doesn't mean that you should now treat your book as a vehicle to dump your sales materials. People view books as a source of education and wisdom. Which means you need to educate your readers. If you fail to do this, expect a huge backlash.

Your book will not only fail to build your authority, it could damage your reputation. The best advice I can give here is never to hold back. Give away your best information to make the best impression.

I see too many authors hold back. They fear giving away everything. Because why would anyone then want to take up their higher-priced services or products if their best advice is in the book?

Remember from Chapter 1 that there are only two types of problems in the world; information problems and motivation problems. Most people think they have an information problem. If they could just find the right words of advice, they could solve their problem.

But the truth is, most people's problems are motivational.

Never fear including your very best advice in your book. Your dream clients need you to motivate them and keep them accountable. Your words of wisdom in a book will never be enough.

Use this insider secret to your advantage. Giving away the very best knowledge you have will mean your book beats all those authors who held back.

Feature Key People

While planning your book, draw up a list of people you could feature. There are two key reasons why it's a good idea to feature other people in your book.

Firstly, if you've found resources to help your audience, adding them into your book will make them appreciate you more. For example, a life coach whose audience is quite spiritual may choose to spotlight a great meditation practitioner.

Secondly, by promoting other people, you can tap into their existing clients and networks. This is without appearing like you are poaching from them.

When you feature someone in your book, they're likely to see it as an honor. You'll find they'll promote your book to their clients, on their website, on social media platforms, etc. This is because being featured in a book increases their authority and credibility.

This is also a fantastic way to keep their clients happy by giving new and useful information, without doing any work themselves.

In other words, by shining a spotlight on others you effectively get others to market your business for you.

> **Warning**
>
> Do not feature people for the sake of it. Yes, you know the secret. Authority-building books are designed to sell you and your business or organization. But the whole point is they are a covert selling mechanism. Featuring people who are not a natural fit gives the game away.
>
> Anyone featured in your book must be aligned to your book's purpose and give value to your readers.

Your Unique Angle or Positioning

At this stage, you have assessed your abilities and interests, your readers' needs, a selection of successful books on your subject, and how to bring it to life using your personality and experiences.

This should allow you to come up with your unique angle or position on this subject.

Four Steps to a Unique Voice Masterclass

Finding a unique voice can be a challenge if you're in a crowded and competitive market. A quick search on Amazon can bring up a ton of different books already written on your subject matter. It's easy for you to believe that it's "all been done before."

Don't be disheartened. I put together a masterclass that shows you the four steps you need to create a unique voice and angle for your book, even if you're in a saturated marketplace.

Even better is that once you dial this in, you will have a unique positioning that you can use not just for your book but for every kind of content you need, such as social media, blog posts, adverts and press releases.

You'll never have to worry about sounding like anyone else ever again. Find details of this masterclass here:

- www.thefreedommasterplan.com/4-steps-masterclass

List Readers' Needs

While researching your book angle you will develop a good idea of what you could, should, might and definitely will put in your book. Now, it's time to tighten that up and learn how to plan a great book outline.

You start that process by listing the readers' needs which you plan to meet. There will be an overall high-level reader need. It covers the main purpose of your book. Each chapter should then meet a lower-level reader need.

Remember, you're teaching them how to create a useful result in every single chapter too.

Helpful Tip

If you have time, I recommend you also create a list of readers' needs for each major point you plan to include.

This means you can always see your information through your typical reader's eyes and make sure they will find value in it. This is a simple but effective 'insurance policy' to help you write a fantastic book that is a credit to your name. Why? You've probably been to a party and stood next to someone who droned on and on about what they were interested in.

Remember how you felt. Chances are you felt bored, frustrated and trapped. Desperately looking for an opportunity to politely escape that pompous windbag.

The 'crashing bore' simply had no interest in what mattered to you, only what mattered to them. The same thing applies to tedious, vanity-project books, only published to boost the author's ego.

By focusing on meeting your readers' needs, you avoid 'crashing bore' syndrome befalling your book.

Instead, you'll have your readers hanging on your every word, enthralled and eager to learn.

Create Your Mind Map

With your readers' needs defined, you can plan how to meet them with your take on your subject. This will become your book outline, ready to expand upon.

The quickest and easiest way to define your outline is to create a mind map. A mind map is a graphical way to represent ideas and concepts. This is a visual thinking tool that helps you analyze and structure information.

Take a look at this example:

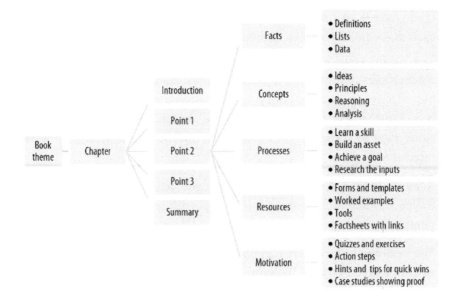

Figure 7: Chapter Mind Map Example

A mind map can also create what I call the 'connect the dots book writing' experience.

As a child, I used to enjoy doing 'connect the dots' worksheets at school. I was never very good at drawing, but with these worksheets I could create beautiful pictures by connecting one dot to the next.

Creating a mind map book outline like this allows you to create a visual template for your book. Once you complete the outline, it's a simple case of going into each section and elaborating on that particular point.

This is what I mean about connect the dots book writing. You go from one section to the next, explaining each point. Once done, you 'connect up' all the sections. No accidentally repeating yourself, no overwhelm, no procrastination and no mistakes.

You can create mind maps online. Just search for mind mapping software on Google.

Alternatively, you can use a pen and paper.

1. Start in the middle of a blank page or screen and add your main reader need topic.

2. Include the related subtopics around this central theme, in a logical sequence, connecting each of them to the center with a line.

3. Repeat the same process for the subtopics, generating lower-level details as you see fit, connecting them to their parent topic too.

4. Analyze your outline's scope and sequence and check it is logical, complete and meets specific readers' needs.

5. Make any adjustments as necessary and double-check it is error free.

Helpful Tip

I recommend you use a free online tool:

- www.mind42.com

It allows you to drag, drop, cut, copy and paste your ideas as you refine them. It's very flexible. When you are happy with it, you can export your mind map as a document. This document has all the headings you need as placeholders, ready for you to expand on. This is a brilliant time-saving technique for writing your book.

You can export your mind map in diagram format too, which is a handy reference guide as you write.

Get Feedback on Your Outline

To make sure your idea is fit for purpose, you need to gather feedback on your book's mind map from other people, ideally, people in your target market.

Armed with this information, you can fix any problems with your outline before you expand on it. Show your reviewers your mind map. Get some feedback on the sequence and scope of your outline.

Things to keep in mind:

- Is there anything they feel is missing from your outline that needs adding in?

- Is there anything that needs removing because it is too basic or perhaps too advanced?

Refine Your Outline

Assess your responses and amend your mind map based on the improvements that need making. This technique is a major timesaver for you, both in the writing and reviewing phases.

You'll avoid mountains of rework. You will save a lot of pain writing irrelevant information, which ultimately needs deleting during the editing phase, as your book is 'tightened up' to increase its reader appeal.

The feedback check also gives you confidence and peace of mind that what you're including in your book is of genuine value to your target audience, is complete and is worth expanding on. This guarantees you will use your time effectively and create a well-received book that is up to your professional standards and worthy of your name on the front cover.

It's important to spend some time getting your outline right. A few hours spent perfecting your plan will avoid long days of stress, disappointment, frustration, and worry trying to fix it later.

Learn Plain English Rules

The best advice I can offer is to practice better writing before you expand on your outline.

Many first-time authors worry about their standard of written English. Perhaps they had a bad experience at school with endless criticism from teachers (I know I had many stinging comments about my English over the years).

Perhaps people in your professional career made harsh comments about your written reports. Others worry they write too slowly. They feel getting their ideas on paper will take too long.

Don't let these two potential issues hold you back. Here's how to solve them. The simplest way to improve the quality of your writing is to learn two plain English rules:

1. Always use short sentences.

2. Always use short words.

When authors follow those two rules, their writing becomes clear and concise, and a joy to read. The book's quality and reader value dramatically improve. The beauty of this approach is that these two rules are quick and easy for anyone to learn and apply.

Get into the habit of checking the word count of your sentences. Shorten the longer ones. Also, look for words with three or more syllables and replace them with a shorter one. You'll find using short words and sentences quickly becomes your natural writing style.

People who insist on using long words and sentences come unstuck during the review. Reviewers complain the explanations are clumsy and confusing. Every single sentence needs swapping for its shorter, concise counterpart.

A skilled, professional editor can do this slow, painstaking work for you. Knowing these two plain English rules beforehand will mean a shorter job for your editor (which can save you a lot of money)!

Superfast Writing

The average typing speed is 40 words per minute. The average speaking speed is around 250 words per minute. That's over six times faster.

Unless you're a speedy typist, I strongly recommend you dictate your book. I dictated a 30,000-word book in seven days. You can do the same, as long as you have a detailed book outline that keeps you on track, as explained in the previous section, and you dictate instead of type.

Here are some tried and tested tools:

1. **www.rev.com**

   This is an online transcription service where you can record your voice and then upload the MP3 files for transcription. Costs are around $1.25 per minute of dictation.

2. **www.temi.com**

   If you're on a shoestring budget, you can opt for Temi, which offers machine-based transcription at $0.25 per minute.

   As there are no humans involved, accuracy is not as great as rev.com, but worth checking out, especially if you don't have a thick accent.

3. **www.otter.ai**

   Otter is a speech-to-text transcription tool that uses artificial intelligence and machine learning. There's a phone app and website. I found it to be accurate, but as with Temi, be aware that thick accents will affect the quality of transcriptions.

   Costs are very fair. As of publishing this book, you get a free trial of 600 minutes transcribed per month. I would test it to see if you like it. If you choose to upgrade, monthly subscriptions are under $10 per month for a huge 6,000-minute plan.

Helpful Tip

Make lots of short recordings. Record each sub-section of your chapters separately. If something goes wrong with a recording, you won't have a whole chapter to re-dictate.

The other great reason is that if you choose human transcription, you can send finished recordings to transcribe while dictating other parts of the book. No waiting around.

Warning

Do not use live voice dictation tools, such as Google Docs Voice Typing. These are tools that type as you talk.

It is difficult to resist the urge to go back and edit your words as you dictate. They're on the screen right in front of you, begging to be edited! I see so many would-be authors cripple themselves by editing while they are writing their books. It's much more productive for you to first pull the whole book out of you. Then you can go back and make edits.

Learn About Readability

You may be surprised to discover that the average reading age of adults in the UK or the US is 12-14 years old. Not 21. You need to make sure that your writing is suitable for the average reading age.

This doesn't mean 'dumbing down' your information. It means making it clear and simple. You don't want your ideas to be exhausting to understand.

If your reader feels like they are wading through insurance small print, they won't thank you for it. They'll write a stinging negative review.

You want your concepts to be quick and easy to enjoy.

Helpful Tip

You can test your readability and the required reading age to understand it, by going to a free website:

- www.read-able.com

Take a paragraph or two of your text and simply paste into the big form field on the website. It will assess it in seconds and give you the required reading age. Double-check your writing meets the 12-14-year-old level. It also gives useful statistics, such as:

- total number of sentences in a paragraph (longer paragraphs are less readable)
- sentence length
- word complexity

This will quickly show you if a paragraph, sentence or word length is bumping up the reading age.

It's okay to have a few sentences where the reading age is higher than the average, but the overall standard you're aiming for must be 12-14 years old.

The fiction writer with the most readable text is the respected Ernest Hemingway. Tim Ferriss, one of the best nonfiction writers, has one of the lowest required reading ages and still has a string of bestsellers to his name.

Readers will skim a paragraph or two when they pick up your book to 'see how it reads.' If that sample is clunky and difficult to grasp, they'll put your book straight back down, and you lose the sale. Clearly an outcome any author worth their salt should avoid at all costs.

Stress-Free Book Sales

This step is second only to the purpose of your book.

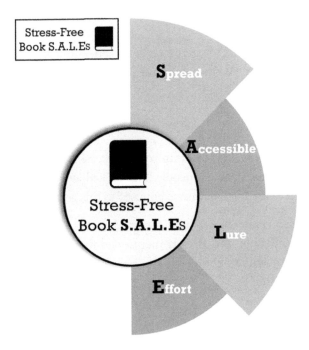

Figure 8: Stress-Free Book S.A.L.Es

One of the brilliant things you discovered inside The Freedom Master Plan is that your book can be a fantastic lead generation tool. For this to happen, you need to lure your readers away from your book periodically.

You need to take them to a website or landing page to capture their contact details. The way to do that is to entice them with something of value.

The good news is, you don't need to come up with new materials most of the time.

In your business right now, you use forms, templates, workbooks, checklists and other materials with your clients. These can be placed online and offered in exchange for a reader to give you their contact details.

Also, look at creating valuable items that you can repurpose later. For example, perhaps you're planning to create a self-paced program at a later date. It would make sense for you to make an MP3, online video, etc., that expands on your book's particular topic. Yes, this takes time, but you're accomplishing two things simultaneously.

You're creating something of value that gets readers to come to your website and leave their details. At the same time, you're building a component of a brilliant Passive Income Asset.

Helpful Tip

If you decide to feature key people in your book, ask them for help. You'll be amazed at how much content people have tucked away. Most are only too happy for you to use these 'exclusive bonuses' as this gets them free publicity.

You could also create an online video, podcast or CD where you interview your key people. You already mentioned them in your book. Many of your readers would be interested to hear more 'exclusive, not-found-in-the-book' content.

Warning

Make sure you drive people to *your* website.

Don't push your readers directly to your key people as you cannot capture the readers' details. In that case, you're now building someone else's list, not yours.

There are four main rules to making sure you max out the leads and sales from your book.

Rule 1: Spread Your Offers Throughout Your Book

Don't do what some authors do and only have a resources list at the back of the book. By all means, have a resources list (I added one to this book). But this should be a handy list summarizing all the offers made throughout the book.

Lists at the back are like glossaries. People rarely read them. You win more eyeballs by having offers spread throughout your book.

You can add offers directly within your content, as well as using boxes to 'call out' offers. See my previous chapters to see how I accomplished this and copy me.

Choosing offers that fit each chapter topic makes them far more compelling. Feel free to go back for some inspiration.

Rule 2: Be Accessible to Your Audience

Some people really don't like clicking on links. Offer other ways for a reader to leave their details, such as phone or e-mail address. Alternative options mean a broader set of readers will contact you.

Rule 3: Lure Your Leads With Different Free and Paid Offers

If you have only one offer, you're limiting yourself. Different offers appeal to different people, maximizing the number of readers who leave you their contact details.

Rule 4: Tailor the Effort Levels

This is a subtle yet powerful strategy. If you have one purpose for your book (e.g., finding dream clients), you don't need this strategy. But this strategy is brilliant if you have one main purpose and one or two smaller purposes. Let me explain.

Let's say your main purpose is to attract dream clients. But you also have an online self-paced program for those who can't afford your higher-ticket products or services.

For your self-paced program, I would advise you to make it as easy as possible for people to contact you. Landing pages capturing name and e-mail address are great.

Or you can try other 'low-effort' ideas such as sending a quick text saying 'yes' to a pre-approved number.

For your higher-priced offers, make it harder for someone to contact you. By adding some difficulty, you add a screening process that weeds out time-wasters and tire-kickers.

Some ideas are asking them to send you an e-mail and answer one or two questions. Or you could drive them to a landing page that hosts a screening questionnaire or application form.

You'll find that by making it harder for these people to contact you, you earn a higher quality of potential clients.

Again, if you need examples, you need look no further than this book (plus the Resources section at the end).

Start Writing

Vast opportunities await you once you're a published author. While your peers slog it out, you can use the shortcut to higher profits and authority. Doing nothing now is like being given the latest lottery ticket numbers and deciding not to play.

Yes, you will have to invest time, effort and money. But I guarantee it will be one of the best business investments you'll ever make. People hand over thousands for a flashy website. Yes, it's a necessary asset. But everyone has one. How many are published authors?

The leverage you'll earn from your authority-building book leaves any website eating dust. Isn't that worth at least the same time, effort and money taken to design your business website?

Stop with the self-doubt. Shut down that little voice telling you that you can't do it. You *can* do it. All it takes is for you to start.

There's no more for me to tell you. All that's left is for you to start writing. Just go for it and don't be too hard on yourself.

I'll leave you with a motivating quote that helped me when I wrote my first book. "You will never win if you never begin."

> *You will never win if you never begin.*
> *(Helen Rowland)*

CAN YOU HELP US?

If you have a moment, please leave me an Amazon review. Share your thoughts at:

- getbook.at/TheFreedomMasterPlan

It will automatically take you to the correct Amazon platform for your country.

Reviews are the lifeblood of any book. It's how platforms like Amazon decide whether to promote a book in their search engine or not.

I need your help to get this book into the hands of as many vegan, plant-based, ethical, sustainable, B Corp, cruelty-free, eco-conscious and social experts, influencers and entrepreneurs as possible, incredible people just like you who are working toward a kinder world.

Help my mission to create an army of conscious, ethical thought leaders through publishing, amplifying our collective voices, so our desire to end the exploitation of animals, humans, and the environment will become too loud to be ignored.

My ultimate dream is to die in a vegan-normal world, where caring for the rights of animals, the environment, and the overall physical and mental health of humans is no longer a fringe movement.

You'll know by now that the fastest way to create vegan and ethical thought leaders is to create published authors who know how to leverage their books for visibility and authority.

I've met so many people whose views on animals, health and the climate were changed permanently after reading a book. That's the power of books.

Your review will help get this book to more people just like you, so they feel empowered to tell their stories.

Together, we can change the world, one book at a time. So please go to the link above and leave your review.

I appreciate you.

RECOMMENDED READING LIST

Sinek, Simon. *Start With Why*, USA: Penguin, 2011.

Skrob, Robert. *The Official Get Rich Guide To Information Marketing*, USA: Entrepreneur Press, 2011.

Skrob, Robert and Regnerus, Bob. *The Official Get Rich Guide To Information Marketing On The Internet*, USA: Entrepreneur Press, 2008.

Dunn, Ken. *The Greatest Prospector in the World*, USA: Next Century Publishing, 2016.

McDonald, Jason. *Social Media Marketing Workbook*, USA: CreateSpace Independent Publishing Platform, 2016.

RESOURCES

At the beginning of this book, I gave you details of two free gifts designed to get your book to market as fast and professionally as possible. Find them both here:

- www.thefreedommasterplan.com

5 Steps to Writing and Publishing Your Business Book PDF:

If you're overwhelmed, have been struck with imposter syndrome, or you just want to get your book out ASAP, without cutting corners, this no-nonsense roadmap will show you how to write and self-publish your book to traditional publishing standards.

21 Essential Questions You Must Ask a Nonfiction Business Book Publisher Before Signing a Contract

If you're confused if you should self-publish or pitch to traditional publishers, and you're afraid you'll make the wrong choice costing you time, energy and money, this manual cuts through the noise and allows you to make the best publishing decision for you.

Throughout this book, I've given you details of resources that help you implement the ideas in the book quickly and precisely. Find them all here:

- www.thefreedommasterplan.com/free-resources

Here's a list of them all and how they help you succeed.

Dream Client PDF Worksheet

If you only want to work with great clients, you need to become crystal clear on who they are. To help you identify them, use this worksheet I've put together for you.

Passive Income Assets PDF Mind Map

Get this handy mind map that shows you the different Passive Income Assets you can create from a business book. This will motivate you to build these profitable residual income streams.

Infinite Content Machine PDF Mind Map

This at-a-glance mind map shows you all the different ways you can repurpose content from your book, so you never run out of content ideas for social media and online marketing.

Direct Mail Ideas PDF Report

Direct mail works. Period. But what dramatically increases conversions are ideas that tie in with your book. Check out these great ideas for authors.

Authority Catalyst PDF Speech Template

Giving memorable speeches will dramatically boost your authority, marking you as a thought leader. This template will give you the confidence you need even if you've never given a speech before.

Other Resources Mentioned in This Book

- www.mind42.com - free online tool that allows you to create full book mind maps.
- www.read-able.com - free online tool that allows you to test how readable your writing is and the required reading age to understand it.
- www.rev.com - online transcription service where you can record your voice and then upload the MP3 files to have them transcribed. Costs are around $1.25 per minute of dictation.

- www.temi.com - machine-based transcription at $0.25 per minute.
- www.otter.ai - speech-to-text transcription tool at a monthly subscription of under $10 per month for up to 6,000 minutes of dictation.
- Four Steps to a Unique Voice - a one-hour masterclass that helps anyone create a unique voice and angle for their book, even in a crowded and competitive marketplace with many books already written on that subject matter:

  - https://thefreedommasterplan.com/4-steps-masterclass

- The Ultimate Press Pack Toolkit for New Authors - industry-standard templates to build a professional media and press pack, with worked examples and the What to Do When You Can't Afford a Publicist book:

  - www.theveganpublisher.com/press-pack-toolkit

NEED MORE HELP?

Complimentary 15-minute Book Breakthrough Consultation

Writing and publishing a book can feel like a daunting task. If you're unsure how to get started, or perhaps you've made a start but are now 'lost' inside your book, I'd love to help you gain clarity.

I usually charge for my breakthrough consultations, but as the owner of a copy of The Freedom Master Plan, I can offer you a free consultation to help you:

- brainstorm book ideas
- analyze your next steps
- create a plan of action
- brainstorm strategies to help you leverage your book (for both existing and would-be authors)

To get started, help me by filling this short questionnaire:

- www.thefreedommasterplan.com/free-consult

If you prefer, e-mail to receive the questionnaire:

- mitali@thefreedommasterplan.com

This is *not* for:

- those who have partially written a book
- those who wish to write fiction, personal memoirs, children's books, academic text books and biographies

INSPIRE OTHERS WITH ONE QUESTION

As a vegan or ethical expert, influencer or entrepreneur, you're already inspiring others to adopt mindful lifestyles that protect and support our environment and its inhabitants, human and non-human.

I'm sure, however, just like me, sometimes it's felt like an uphill battle convincing others to adopt kinder lifestyles, even when doing so would lead to better health.

I know several people suffering from chronic illnesses such as type 2 diabetes, heart disease and high cholesterol. They could eradicate these diseases by becoming plant-based.

But food companies and animal agriculture have deep pockets. They can advertise and convince our loved ones that consuming animal products is good for them.

In the introduction to this book, I spoke about the Big Tobacco lawsuit in the early noughties. Decades ago, tobacco companies convinced our grandparents and great-grandparents that smoking was healthy for their lungs and even helped in sports (for example, there are old photos of cyclists smoking while participating in the Tour De France competition).

These food companies are doing exactly what tobacco companies did decades ago. What chance do we have to convince our loved ones they don't have to suffer when we're up against giant corporates?

It's why I breathed a sigh of relief when I met Peter Goldstein from weDIDit. Health.

He's building a whole movement focused on bringing Hippocrates' truth, "Let food be thy medicine," into the mainstream.

His goal is to save trillions of dollars currently spent in the sick-care system and save billions of lives.

weDIDit.Health recently launched the Million Healthy Lives Challenge to show the world that a whole-food, plant-based lifestyle has a huge impact on health. It provides actual evidence that there is a real solution to chronic disease.

When our loved ones see how many people, like themselves, have reduced their suffering, they're far more likely to make necessary changes.

And more people becoming plant-based means a sustainable planet and a kinder world for animals too. A real win-win-win!

I'm proud to be one of Peter's ambassadors, and I urge you to join us. You could improve the health of others by simply answering one question - go here and answer it:

- https://wedidit.health

KEEP IN TOUCH!

Your success means the world to me and I hope you enjoyed discovering how writing and publishing a business book achieves the freedom you want in your business.

When you gain freedom from all the typical problems business owners have and start making the profits you deserve, you get to concentrate on the real reason you started your business or organization. Ending the exploitation of animals, humans and the environment.

You can do this. I wish you every success touching as many lives as possible (human and non-human).

Please do share your success stories with me. I'd love to hear from you. E-mail them to:

- mitali@thefreedommasterplan.com

All the best with your plan,

Mitali

QUIZ ANSWERS

1. Define Celebrity Halo:
   - ☐ The need to become a celebrity at all costs.
   - ☐ Creating fan fiction of your favorite celebrity.
   - ☑ The urge to be associated with and bask in the reflected glory of a celebrity.

2. Which is correct? You can leverage your business book to:
   - ☐ Find great coaches.
   - ☑ Find dream clients.
   - ☐ Find great software.

3. Which of these is *not* one of the steps inside the Referral Revenue Engine?
   - ☐ Free book giveaway
   - ☑ Price your book as high as you can.
   - ☐ Feature well-connected strategic partners.

Chapter 2

1. The more income you make, the more it is about…

   ☐   How good you are at a particular skill.

   ☑   Who you are and not how good you are at a particular skill.

   ☐   How many qualifications you have.

2. Which two below are Passive Income Assets?

   ☑   Self-paced program.

   ☑   Subscription.

   ☐   Speaking engagement.

3. What are the two types of subscriptions?

   ☐   Audiobooks and self-paced programs.

   ☐   E-books and audiobooks.

   ☑   Monthly membership programs and done-for-you services.

Chapter 3

1. What is Diagnostic Selling?
   - ☑ Eliminating selling by having the authority to diagnose instead.
   - ☐ Immediately getting more sales calls.
   - ☐ Never having to speak to potential clients on the phone again.

2. What can eliminate sales anxiety for good?
   - ☑ Your authority-building book.
   - ☐ An incredible salesperson that you hire.
   - ☐ A great website that sells your services.

3. At which sales phase can you use the Zero Selling System?
   - ☐ Just pre-sale.
   - ☑ Pre-sale, peri-sale (during) and post-sale.
   - ☐ Pre-sale and post-sale.

Chapter 4

1. What is the sexiest word in the English Language?
   - ☑ Free.
   - ☐ You.
   - ☐ Buy.

2. What is an Infinite Content Machine?
   - ☐ An outsourced company that creates all your content for you.
   - ☑ Leveraging a book to create content once and then never needing to create again.
   - ☐ Needing to create content infinitely for social media.

3. Which of these is *not* one of the steps inside the Media Machine?
   - ☐ Ask for endorsements.
   - ☐ Start local.
   - ☑ Only focus on traditional media.

Chapter 5

1. Define Authority Catalyst:
   - ☐ Giving away books at record speed to get respect and recognition.
   - ☑ Using public speaking as a way to get accelerated respect and recognition.
   - ☐ Getting bestseller status to get respect and recognition.

2. Which of these is *not* a Get Gigs step?
   - ☐ Prove you can generate publicity for the promoter.
   - ☑ Refuse to bring extra value to the promoter.
   - ☐ Make an impact on the promoter's objectives.

3. Which of these is *not* a virtue?
   - ☑ Modesty.
   - ☐ Patience.
   - ☐ Integrity.

Printed in Great Britain
by Amazon

21173497R00103